RESPONDING
TO AMERICA'S HOMELESS

RESPONDING TO AMERICA'S HOMELESS
Public Policy Alternatives

F. Stevens Redburn and Terry F. Buss

PRAEGER

New York
Westport, Connecticut
London

Library of Congress Cataloging-in-Publication Data

Redburn, F. Stevens.
  Responding to America's homeless.

  Bibliography: p.
    1. Homelessness—United States.   2. Homelessness—
Government policy—United States.   3. Domicile in
public welfare—United States.   I. Buss, Terry F.
II. Title.
HV4505.R43   1986   362.5'0973   86-21186
ISBN 0-275-92231-6 (alk. paper)

Library of Congress Catalog Card Number: 86-21186

ISBN: 0-275-92231-6

First published in 1986

Praeger Publishers, One Madison Avenue, New York, NY 10010
A division of Greenwood Press, Inc.

Printed in the United States of America

The paper used in this book complies with the
Permanent Paper Standard issued by the National
Information Standards Organization (Z39.48-1984).

10   9   8   7   6   5   4   3   2

For
Mary Ann Redburn
and
Carla Wilson Buss

CONTENTS

LIST OF TABLES

LIST OF FIGURES

PREFACE

In undertaking this work, we were quite conscious of the emotions that surround discussions of homelessness and of the limited, although rapidly growing, base of careful research on which to draw. Indeed, the opportunity to improve the ratio of information to emotion in such discussions was a major motive for the project.

As recently as 1983, only scattered systematic research was available, from a handful of localized studies, on the extent and nature of homelessness in the United States. With publication of the U.S. Department of Housing and Urban Development's national report on homelessness and emergency shelters in early 1984, and completion of the first statewide systematic survey of homeless people themselves by the Ohio Department of Mental Health in the same year, the picture changed. Now, basic information was available on numbers, distribution, causes, needs, and how those needs were being addressed across the country. And now, a broad cross section of the homeless population had been interviewed directly regarding their personal backgrounds, present circumstances, and state of body and mind. The availability of this new information led us to begin a book that, we believed, could provide reasonable guidance to policymakers and others concerned with the homeless.

The first author was a member of the HUD research team that produced the 1984 report. The second author helped to design and carry out the Ohio survey and contributed to the survey report. However, the interpretations we make of HUD's published findings and the analyses and conclusions we draw from the Ohio data are strictly our own. Similarly, the opinions we express in the latter chapters regarding current public policies and future policy alternatives are our own thoughts and may or may not be consistent with the official positions of any government agency.

Our analyses have led us to take a more differentiated view of the homeless than previously and to recognize the need for new public policies that aim to do more than meet immediate needs for emergency food and shelter. If others gain as much insight into these issues from reading these pages as we have gained in writing them, then our original intention will be fulfilled.

ACKNOWLEDGMENTS

Although we have drawn on a wide variety of data sources in preparing this manuscript, our analysis would not have been possible without data provided by the Ohio Department of Mental Health (ODMH) from its study of Ohio's homeless conducted for the National Institute of Mental Health.* We would especially like to thank Pam Hyde, director of ODMH and Dee Roth, chief of Program Evaluation and Research, for their cooperation and encouragement.

This project was made possible through the data-gathering and data-processing efforts of dozens of people. We are particularly indebted to two people. Yvonne Simon conducted all of the case study interviews and more than 100 personal interviews for the study of homelessness in Ohio. She repeatedly ventured into the most dangerous areas of several Ohio cities to gather information from people who have every incentive to remain silent; she is quite simply the best interviewer anywhere. We are also indebted to Jerry Bean of ODMH for providing us with his expert analysis and interpretation of the psychological status of homeless people for Chapter 5.

The project received clerical and technical support from various departments at Youngstown State University (YSU). Judith Ferrett of the Center for Urban Studies expertly and efficiently typed and corrected the manuscript in its many drafts and revisions. Media Center technicians and artists, especially Mary Ann Bodnark, Carl Leet, and Denise Donnan, were responsible for producing excellent graphics. Hildegard Schnuttgen and Debbie Beronja of the Reference Department of Maag Library were very helpful in locating and acquiring many references. Staff members at the YSU Computer Center, particularly Fred Ullom and Tom Davidson, helped with data processing. Julie DeGalan of the Center for Urban Studies expertly and quickly developed the computer programs necessary for data analyses.

The manuscript benefited a great deal from the comments and criticism of policy analysts and administrators who examined our drafts. Deserving of special mention are Roger Vaughan, Dee Roth, C. Richard Hofstetter, Anne Lezak

---

*The Ohio study was funded by the National Institute of Mental Health, grant no. 1R18 MH38877-01, to the Office of Program Evaluation and Research, Ohio Department of Mental Health. Dee Roth served as principal investigator on the project.

and Irene Shifrin Levine of the National Institute of Mental Health, Marty Abravanel, Deborah Devine, and Barbara Dyer. Like others who work with these issues, we owe a special debt to Kathleeen Peroff, who directed the first major national study of the homeless, in 1984, for the U.S. Department of Housing and Urban Development. Kathy assisted us in preparing the book's seventh chapter and offered comments on other parts of the manuscript. The authors, of course, bear sole responsibility for the contents and conclusions.

Finally, we would like to thank Catherine Woods and Michael Fisher at Praeger Publishers for their support and encouragement.

RESPONDING
TO AMERICA'S HOMELESS

1

INTRODUCTION

In Washington, D.C., at dawn on a cold winter morning, one man finds another lying on a bus shelter bench. The man on the bench shows signs of life; but by the time help reaches him he is dead.

A woman and her three children sit in Chicago's train station. They are not waiting for a train. They have been there for days. They have nowhere to go.

Each winter night, New York's city government shelters over 8,000 single adults and provides emergency housing in shelters and hotel rooms for more than 4,000 families. The city claims it spends more dollars per capita than any other to aid the homeless; but advocates for the homeless maintain that the typical, large city-run shelter is dangerous and inhumane.

In Los Angeles and its suburbs, an estimated 30,000 people cannot go home at night. They, like thousands of others in communities across this wealthy nation, have no homes.

In modern societies, a permanent residence is regarded as normal and necessary. To be without a place called home is seen by most as one of the severest forms of human deprivation or deviance. Yet, there are many homeless people in even the most affluent societies; and their numbers appear to be growing in the United States as in other industrialized countries.[1]

The numbers of homeless fluctuate over the years for reasons not fully understood. In the United States, a surge of homeless people coincided with the Great Depression of the 1930s, as young single men drifted in search of work and families lost their homes or farms and went on the road. Their homelessness was seen by most as part of the more general economic problem and, to the extent it was a public policy concern, as something to treat as part of the general effort to relieve hardship and revive the nation's cconomy. The other homeless—the hobos and vagabonds who would have been homeless in better times—were not considered a proper focus of public policy, except perhaps by local police.

Today, homelessness has been rediscovered as a social problem distinct from the broader problems of persistent poverty, unemployment, and social deviance. The homeless are perceived as a group with distinctive characteristics and problems. Their visibility and political significance have reached a modern high point.

In the United States, new public attention to the homeless has been accompanied by a major expansion of emergency shelter and other services for them, by a new effort to understand the causes of homelessness and the needs of the homeless, and by experimentation with public policies to reduce if not eliminate the hardships suffered by the homeless.

Whether this new concern leads to effective public action depends not only on the depth of our commitment, however, but also on our ability to devise new ways of dealing with homeless people based on an improved understanding of who they are and what they want and need.

The causes of homelessness today are less obvious than they were, or were assumed to be, during the Depression; and, despite our heightened awareness, we understand how to deal with homelessness no better than in the past. The first systematic estimates of the scope of the problem in various parts of the country and of other basic facts about the homeless and the nation's emergency shelter system were not made until 1984 (U.S. Department of Housing and Urban Development 1984). In that year, also, the first large-scale representative in-person survey was taken among a state's homeless population (Ohio Department of Mental Health 1985). These two studies, when combined with the insights gained from other recent empirical work on the homeless, provide a minimal foundation of knowledge for effective public action.

QUESTIONS

Before we can act wisely, we must see clearly the nature of homelessness. We also must think clearly about what we want for the homeless and how to get it. The first part of this book (Chapters 2 through 6) brings new information and original analysis to the questions of who the homeless are, how they survive, how they have come to their present condition, and what they need.

With the information recently made available, we can address some basic questions that heretofore have had no answers:

1. How many are homeless at any give time?
2. What are their demographic characteristics?
3. Where are the homeless, and what are their patterns of movement?

4. How, and with what degree of success, do the homeless meet their basic needs for food and shelter?

In addition, we can now explore the complex questions of etiology:

5. By what chains of events do people become homeless?
6. Why are some people unable, and others unwilling, to maintain a regular, permanent residence?
7. How many of the homeless suffer from severe mental illness or other chronic disabling conditions?

And, we can examine questions regarding the needs of this population:

8. How many of the homeless are capable of independent living?
9. To what extent is it realistic to aim at the elimination of homelessness and reintegration of homeless people into the social mainstream?

The second part of the book (Chapters 7 and 8) looks at what is currently being done to help meet basic needs of the homeless and explores alternatives to current public policies.

By reviewing information about what private groups and governments have done for the homeless, it is possible to answer such questions as these:

10. What services are available to and used by the homeless in various parts of the country?
11. How effectively are current government programs and privately sponsored efforts on behalf of homeless people meeting their immediate and longer-run needs for shelter?

Finally, drawing together a variety of evidence about the nature of homelessness and the current direction of efforts to help, it is possible to critically analyze that direction and propose alternatives. This final step in the analysis addresses questions such as these:

12. By what standards should the success of a public policy on homelessness be judged?
13. What controls, if any, can legitimately be imposed on homeless people in order to protect them from harm?
14. Beyond meeting their obvious need for shelter, what should be done about the homeless?

These questions are elaborated in the remainder of this chapter and explored systematically throughout the book. Because of the strong emotions raised by homelessness and the limits of our information, the answers offered based on

an interpretation of available evidence are likely to be disputed—a welcome debate if it furthers scientific inquiry and understanding of the troubling phenomenon of people who have no home.

THE NATURE OF HOMELESSNESS

In a society that collects so many statistics—on matters as diverse as base-
ball and building permits—it is startling that no reliable national statistics exist
on the number of homeless people. We cannot even be sure (although the weight
of evidence suggests it) that the number of homeless people is greater today than
it was five or ten years ago. At least, a reliable count would allow us to compare the approximate number of homeless people with the number of emergency
shelter spaces, indicating the adequacy of current efforts to provide shelter.

The first systematic national study of the homeless addressing the issue of
numbers was carried out by the U.S. Department of Housing and Urban Development in January 1984 (U.S. Department of Housing and Urban Development
1984). It yielded estimates far lower than those offered by advocates for the
homeless and commonly cited by the press. HUD's effort produced bitter attacks.
Some condemned the motives, methods, and conclusions of the government
study. But, despite the intensity of reaction, HUD's report stands as the only
source of reliable information on how many homeless there are nationally, how
they are distributed geographically, what their characteristics are, how they came
to be homeless, and what shelter services are available to them.

Changing Views of the Homeless

In the last few years, there has been a shift of opinion regarding the nature,
causes, and social significance of homelessness. Perhaps this reflects a real
historic shift in the nature and significance of the phenomenon; and possibly it
reflects changes in the way organized interests and the media interpret the phenomenon. In any case, there are different and partially incompatible views (with
differing policy implications) concerning who the homeless are, how they became that way, and what this tells us about the nature of the society.

The two dominant traditional American stereotypes of homeless people are
"the vagabond" and "the vagrant." Both are seen as people who, either through
personal misfortune or by choice, have taken to the roads, the rails, or the city
streets. But, in both cases, homelessness has become, for them, a way of life.

From the viewpoint of the larger society, and as labeled by sociologists, these
homeless are culturally "deviant"; that is, they and their way of living are stig-
matized by most people, even as they are pitied or envied by some. The vagabond or wanderer is more likely to be envied for having escaped the spiritual

domestication of conventional society; he (the stereotype is usually represented as male) is seen as a rebel, a misfit, and an outcast (Himmelfarb 1984, pp. 317–46). The vagrant is more likely to be pitied as someone unable to cope with normal society, a "bum," probably a "wino," either unwilling to get or unable to hold a steady job. "Skid row" and the "hobo jungle" are his haunts.

Society owes little to the vagabond, since he has chosen to live "outside." The vagrant may not be a volunteer but is, very likely, a "lost cause." Although churches might feed such people and try to save their souls, no public programs would be launched to bring them back into society. Only when hard times added greatly to their numbers and increased the potential for disorder or assaults on the sensibilities of normal society, would governments act either to provide emergency food and shelter or to drive them away.

Both of these stereotypes have been around for a long time. During the Depression, large numbers of wandering and desperate men reinforced both images. In the 1960s, the relaxation of convention and emergence of a highly mobile subculture of footloose youth reinforced and updated our image of the vagabond. That many now regard both "vagrant" and "vagabond" as stereotypes suggests that, for whatever reason, they no longer are consistent with much that we see and hear about today's homeless. Our views are still in flux; and additional information, especially that provided by systematic studies, may lead us to more complex and accurate as well as more current interpretations. Whether there are, as the media claim, groups of "the new homeless" or merely more and better information about the nature of homelessness, we need to transcend traditional stereotypes in order to act wisely.

Among the "new" groups of homeless discovered by the media are families forced from their homes by job loss, eviction, or cutbacks in public assistance programs; abused women and youthful runaways; and the deinstitutionalized or never-institutionalized mentally ill. But, we have only recently begun to accumulate scientific evidence regarding the relative proportions of homeless in these and other categories.

Causes

In the last 20 years, the resident population of U.S. mental institutions has been reduced by 70 percent. Assuming that the rate of serious mental illness in the population is unchanged since the earlier period, as many as 400,000 people who would have been institutionalized prior to 1965 are today living in community facilities or on their own. However, the current age structure of the population probably places a larger proportion at risk of developing severe chronic mental disorders; thus, the decline in the institutionalization rate may underestimate the number of mentally ill who would have been hospitalized under practices prevailing in the 1950s and 1960s (Bachrach 1982). Although most of the diagnosed mentally ill are technically in community care programs, an unknown number of the severely ill have apparently joined the numbers of those living on the streets or in emergency shelters.

The federal government's Alcohol, Drug Abuse, and Mental Health Administration (ADAMHA) estimated in 1983 that as many as one-half of the homeless suffer from alcohol, drug abuse, or mental health problems (U.S. ADAMHA 1983, 1–6). Such estimates are not based on clinical information, however; nor are the definitional boundaries of mental illness and substance abuse clear-cut. Thus, there is room for disagreement concerning the proportions of the homeless who are severely mentally ill and/or chronically abuse drugs or alcohol.[2] Also, it remains unclear to what extent these problems are primary or contributing causes of the onset of homelessness rather than responses to the severe emotional and physical deprivations produced by living in such a condition.

The acceleration of economic change since 1980 is frequently cited as one reason for the increasing numbers of homeless, especially families. A wave of plant closings and business and farm bankruptcies in that period destroyed the jobs of over 11 million workers (Noble 1986). Although the economy produced new jobs to replace those being eliminated, the more rapid pace of economic change disrupted the lives of more people and put many on the road in search of new opportunities.[3]

Another explanation for the rise of homelessness offered by many observers is the reduction in federal social welfare spending and stricter eligibility requirements for benefit programs imposed during the Reagan years. The households most likely to be affected are those who were already poor or near poor. Thus, the cutbacks (along with the severe recession of 1982-83) produced a sharp rise in the poverty rate that seemed to coincide with reports of increasing homelessness.

The inability to afford housing is another explanation frequently offered for the homelessness of both families and individuals. Although more people than ever are living in subsidized housing, many others who are eligible for such assistance remain on waiting lists for public housing or subsidy certificates that would permit them to rent in the private sector.[4] Where rents are high, some who are fully employed in low-paying jobs may be unable to afford housing within commuting distance of their jobs; this is an especially painful dilemma for those working poor earning enough to be ineligible for federal rent assistance, but not enough to pay local market rents.

Abandonment of low-cost housing or its conversion to higher-income occupancy or other uses also contribute to localized low-income housing shortages. The much praised and publicly subsidized revival of many large cities' central business districts has removed a stock of housing that traditionally provided cheap intermittent lodging to the down and out. In New York City over the last 20 years, more than 30,000 single-room occupancy (SRO) hotel rooms have been lost, through abandonment, demolition, and conversion to more profitable uses.

Other cities (including Denver, San Francisco, Seattle, and Portland) have documented similar losses of cheap transient lodging in old hotels and boarding houses (HUD 1984; Kasinitz 1984).

These and other plausible reasons have been offered for the apparent increase in homelessness over the last five to ten years. While it is certain that each explains some proportion of the increase, it is not clear which are the major and which are relatively minor contributors. Addressing this question is an important step in fashioning new public policies to reduce the incidence of homelessness.

Degrees of Deprivation

Apart from the issue of causation, it will help our understanding of homelessness and its implications if we treat it not as an absolute condition, but as one that varies both in degree and duration. These variations are likely to be correlated with the causes of homelessness discussed above and have important implications for services and other public policies dealing with homelessness. Short-term spells of homelessness are more likely to stem from personal crises or external disasters than from chronic disabling illness, addiction, or poverty. A large minority of the homeless experience recurring episodes of homelessness; for instance, an individual with very limited income may be unable to pay rent for a portion of each month, during which he or she lives on the street or in an emergency shelter.

At the other extreme, a minority of the homeless have been in that condition for two years or more. Many are likely to be people with chronic disabling conditions, which may have led to their homelessness or may have developed later and thus contributed to their remaining in this status. People who are homeless for long periods must adapt in many ways to life without a permanent home or predictable source of shelter. For many of them, homelessness has become a way of life, in the sense that it is an established and routine pattern. Chronic homelessness will have altered their attitudes, behavior, and appearance in ways that would make the return to a normal residence pattern difficult and increasingly unlikely.

Apart from its duration, homelessness varies greatly in degree or severity of deprivation as measured by the nature of temporary shelter to which an individual has access. Using a relatively broad definition that includes anyone without a separate, stable, livable housing unit, the least deprived groups of homeless include those doubling up with family or friends on a temporary basis and those who are able to pay part of the time for predictable lodging at a boarding-house or SRO hotel. Those in emergency shelters or using vouchers to obtain motel, hotel, or other temporary lodging occupy an intermediate category. The homeless who spend most of their time outside or moving from public spaces to abandoned buildings or other makeshift protected locations at night or in bad weather are among the most severely deprived. There is likely to be some correlation between the duration of homelessness and the severity of deprivation measured in terms of access to shelter. Both duration and severity have implications for public action.

PUBLIC POLICY AND THE HOMELESS

> In 1532, the Parliament sentenced beggars to forced labor in chains; in 1534, it warned them to get out of Paris within three days or face hanging; in 1596, the Parliament ordered all vagrants out of the city within twenty-four hours under penalty of being hanged and strangled without benefit of trial (Bernard 1970, p. 133).

Just as views of the homeless have changed, so have society's ways of dealing with them. In recent years, the focus of public policy discussion relative to homelessness has shifted from policing or reforming deviant behavior to meeting obvious needs for protection from weather, for adequate food, and for other modest immediate comforts. And, as the policy debate expands, a broader range of issues and questions emerges.

The major concern of advocates for the homeless in this decade has been to increase and improve the supply of emergency shelters. The need for such increases has been documented by numerous community studies and by the federal government (HUD 1984). Evidence suggests a complex relationship between supply and demand for emergency services. The problem is not simply one of expanding shelter capacity, but of doing so in places and in such a manner so as to ensure that the additional capacity is appropriate for and used by those who most need it.

Beyond Shelter

Providing emergency shelter, in any case, is just the starting point for an adequate public policy to address the needs of homeless people. In fact, commitment to funding a massive permanent system of emergency shelter would amount to accepting, for the indefinite future, the presence of large numbers of homeless people. The recent development of large-scale publicly supported shelter systems in New York City and Washington, D.C., could be the beginnings of a new form of marginal public housing assistance on a continuing basis to people who are otherwise not served by subsidized housing. Before making such a commitment, we should determine whether or not effective policies can be developed for reducing homelessness—ones that the public would endorse and be willing to pay for. These policies could be placed into two categories: *preventive* strategies to reduce the numbers of people becoming homeless, and *correc-*

tive strategies that would return homeless people to permanent housing and otherwise reintegrate them into the community.

Whether preventive or corrective, strategies will prove cost-effective, and what those strategies may consist of are questions addressed in the latter chapters of this book. Adequate answers must be based on sound understanding of homelessness, its causes, and the efficacy of programs and services that might be included in a preventive or corrective strategy.

To define services appropriate to various categories of the homeless, the following must be answered:

• How many of the homeless are unable to live on their own, without supervision, and thus need continuing *custodial* care? Should we, as one observer of the homeless has suggested, revive the nineteenth century concept of "asylums" for such people? Should we, at least partially, reverse the movement toward deinstitutionalization of the mentally ill?

• How many of the homeless are people with some major deficit (a physical handicap, a crippling but correctable psychosocial disorder) whose needs can be met through a program of *developmental* services that will make them socially independent and remove the cause of their homelessness?

• How many of the homeless are victims of temporary misfortune (a fire, a lost job, family violence) who only need short-term *emergency* care while they rebound and find other resources?

• And, how many of those using emergency shelters or other services for the homeless are people who are not homeless by necessity, have no disabling condition, and, given their options, have a lesser claim to these services?[5]

Interwoven with questions such as these, which can be answered with data and analysis, are others that require ethical or legal solutions. The problem situations posed below are representative of the latter.

• Advocates for the homeless have attempted to establish a legal "right to shelter." In November 1984, Washington, D.C. voters passed a referendum, later overturned in court, obligating the city government to shelter all homeless people. By the terms of a 1981 court consent decree, the city of New York remains under a similar obligation. Is the right to shelter one of those basic human rights that are or should be constitutionally guaranteed?

• Local authorities occasionally use force to remove "tent cities" or to disperse concentrations of the homeless considered offending or dangerous. What is the proper balance, in such cases, between the public's health and safety and the needs of these deprived people?

• In early 1985, New York City police began picking up homeless individuals found outside and transporting them for the night to hospitals whenever the wind chill factor fell below five degrees Fahrenheit. Civil liberties attorneys challenged this practice, even though it was undertaken as a life-preserving measure. Under what conditions should coercion be used to protect the homeless from the hazards of life on the streets?

• The federal government and some states and local governments have spent large sums in recent years expanding aid to the homeless. Other states and localities have done relatively little; and some local authorities actively encourage the emigration of homeless people to more hospitable jurisdictions. What level of government should bear primary responsibility for aiding the homeless?

The public policy issues are many and complex. Answers will require a much better understanding of the nature of homelessness, and a reexamination of our assumptions about our obligations toward our most deprived neighbors, and individuals' responsibilities for their own welfare.

NOTES

1. Thomas (1985) summarizes information on homelessness in European countries. Homelessness on an entirely different scale is a feature of many poorer societies. The United Nations has estimated that 100 million people worldwide have no shelter of any kind.

2. A Task Force Report of the American Psychiatric Association (Lamb 1984) noted that study estimates of the incidence of mental illness among homeless groups are highly variable, ranging up to 91 percent (p. 9). See Chapter 5 for discussion of this issue.

3. The rate at which jobs are created and destroyed can be startling to those who mainly focus on relatively stable measures of aggregate gross output or employment. A study of the Cleveland area economy, for instance, showed that, over a two-year period, about 25 percent of the jobs in that economy had disappeared due to business closings or contractions, and had been replaced during that time by a roughly equal number of jobs created by birth of new establishments and expansions of existing operations (Eberts 1984).

4. Although the expansion of federal housing subsidies for the poor has slowed since 1981, the accumulated number of low-income units currently assisted will have increased from 3.2 million in 1981 to 4 million by the end of 1985.

5. Compare Thomas J. Main (1983, 16), who presents evidence that New York's shelters "were drawing on a large pool of higher functioning young men who were not homeless before they came to the shelter."

I

A PORTRAIT OF HOMELESSNESS

—— 2 ——

WHO ARE THE HOMELESS?
Definitions, Numbers, and Demographics

There is widespread agreement in the United States on the moral obligation to help those who are homeless through public or private programs. But a sense of obligation is where this agreement ends. Despite extensive media and public attention given to the homeless beginning about 1983, much of the debate still is over basic factual questions:

- Who should and should not be considered homeless? (a question of definition)
  - How many homeless people are there? (a question of numbers) and
  - Who are the homeless? (a question of demographics)

How these questions are answered will determine how both political leaders and the public view the nature and extent of the homeless problem; and these perceptions, in turn, will help shape public and private responses to homelessness. This chapter attempts to shed some new light on the issues of definitions, numbers, and demographics.

DEFINING HOMELESSNESS

In simple terms, a person is homeless if they do not have a stable, reliable source of housing. Terms that seem straightforward often prove slippery, however, when we try to pin them down. There is considerable room for disagreement over the boundaries of "homelessness"; and broader or narrower definitions of the condition have important implications for how citizens and leaders see and respond to the problem.

A close look at the simple definition offered above reveals two dimensions: place and time. With regard to place, some consider homeless only those who sleep either in emergency shelters or in places not usually used as housing—cars, abandoned buildings, subways, bus or train terminals, a steam grate or doorway, the beach, a cave, woods, a park bench. Others extend the list to include the homes of others (often friends or relatives) or flophouses, single-room occupancy (SRO) hotels, jails, detoxification centers, and migrant worker housing. With regard to time, some consider homelessness to include those sleeping in unconventional or temporary surroundings for brief periods in the wake of a disaster or eviction, while others at least implicitly define homelessness as a living pattern established over a prolonged period of time and sociologically distinct from temporary dislocation. From the former perspective, many people move in and out of a homeless condition, often for short periods; from the latter perspective, homelessness is a long-term phenomenon affecting a much smaller number.

The nature and scale of "homelessness" look very different, depending on how tightly the boundaries of time and place are drawn. A narrow definition conveys the impression that relatively few people are seriously deprived of shelter and understates the extent to which certain kinds of people are thus deprived. A broader definition may blur the distinction between homelessness and the larger problems of inadequate housing and poverty. (Some definitions used in recent studies of the problem are listed in the box below.) There is no correct definition; rather, different definitions have different uses.[1]

SOME DEFINITIONS OF HOMELESSNESS

• *HUD, in its study, classified a person as homeless if he or she slept (1) "in public or private emergency shelters which take a variety of forms—armories, schools, church basements, government buildings, former firehouses and where temporary vouchers are provided by private and public agencies, even hotels, apartments, or boarding homes"; or (2) "in the streets, parks, subways, bus terminals, railroad stations, airports, under bridges or aqueducts, in abandoned buildings without utilities, cars, trucks, or any of the public or private space that is not designed for shelter."*
• *The National Institute of Mental Health (NIMH) proposed a far broader but also vague definition of homelessness, not entirely based on type of shelter: "anyone who lacks adequate shelter, resources, and community ties."*
• *The Community Service Society of New York (a nonprofit human service organization) added to the NIMH definition, "...those whose primary residence is in other well-hidden sites known only to their users."*

- *The U.S. General Accounting Office (1985) used a definition that "encompasses the common components of the above definitions to include: 'those persons who lack resources and community ties necessary to provide for their own adequate shelter.' "*
- *The Ohio Department of Mental Health (1985) was more specific, suggesting that those living in extremely substandard housing such as flophouses or single-room-only (SROs) hotels are homeless if they only have sufficient resources to reside in these places for less than 45 days and consider themselves to be homeless. In addition, the Ohio definition includes those who have been forced to move in with friends and relatives on a temporary basis (also 45 days or less) because they have become homeless.*

HUD's definition is useful for measuring the current level of need for emergency shelters and related services. The Ohio study definition, which is broader than HUD's in terms of place, is perhaps more useful for exploratory research on the nature and causes of homelessness. Casting a broader net permits a more extensive set of comparisons.

Under all definitions, homelessness refers not to an aboslute condition but to a deprivation that varies in degree, depending on the extent to which the location departs from housing that is considered standard, the extent to which the location is temporary or unstable, and the length of time these conditions must be endured. The extent of deprivation also depends on the degree to which homelessness, defined in terms of time and place, is combined with social isolation and material poverty. Within the broader definitional boundaries of homelessness, there are extremely wide variations on each of these dimensions of deprivation. Thus, homelessness is not adequately defined by specifying its outer limits.

Another aspect of the definitional problem that is especially confusing to the media stems from the failure of those who keep statistics and of those who report them to differentiate three common ways of counting: (1) the numbers of people homeless at a single point in time (e.g., on one night); (2) the numbers of homeless over a specified period of time (e.g., over the course of a year); and (3) the total numbers served by or counted by a given agency or group of agencies within a specified period of time. News stories on the homeless commonly mix these numbers, adding confusion to what is already a complicated, difficult, and intensely controversial question: Just how many homeless are there?

COUNTING THE HOMELESS

Perhaps it isn't important whether there are 200,000 homeless in the United States or two million. Perhaps, as homeless advocate Mitch Snyder says, the numbers are only important to "our small, Western minds." Ironically, however, Snyder has been the source of the most widely quoted estimate of the numbers of homeless, which has been repeated endlessly—sometimes as "two million," other times as "2.2 million" or "two to three million." And it has been Snyder who has accused officials of the U.S. Department of Housing and Urban Development of "cooking the numbers" produced by its January 1984 effort to estimate the scope and character of homelessness nationally. HUD's much lower estimates were seen by many as a deliberate attempt by a conservative administration to minimize the problem and fend off efforts to increase public expenditures for the homeless (U.S. Department of Housing and Urban Development 1984).

Although there is no evidence to support Snyder's charge that HUD deliberately undercounted the homeless, he is correct in his political calculation that numbers make a difference. At stake are the public's views of the nature and magnitude of the problem and the scale of government's efforts to deal with it. Unfortunately, counting the homeless is a social scientist's nightmare.

Why Counting is Difficult

The homeless are difficult to count, especially in a society like the United States, because of the way they live and because the usual, address-based, census techniques do not apply.

Need for Invisibility

Homeless people often attempt to remain invisible to improve their prospects for survival in a hostile environment. Those living in abandoned buildings must avoid police who would evict them. Remaining inconspicuous in a bus terminal may allow a homeless person to stay the night in the same way as other people in transit. In the alleyways or back streets, homeless people who mind their own business may be less of a target for those who would commit violent crimes against them. Some homeless may not want to be bothered by social workers and other concerned people who want to help them, preferring their liberty and isolation to social contact. Counting invisible people is difficult.

Hostile Environments

Most direct head counts of the homeless have been performed in shelters or missions. Other estimates are obtained through interviews with human service providers who care for the homeless. Few research efforts, the Ohio study being one exception, have searched out the homeless in other locations such as abandoned buildings, bridges, culverts, alleys, and city parks. These places are dangerous for census takers or interviewers, as they are for the homeless themselves. In the Ohio study, for example, two interviewers were robbed and another was threatened with a knife during interviews (see account following).

COUNTING RURAL HOMELESS IN OHIO

Counting rural homeless people presented some special problems, which help to illustrate some of the difficulties in obtaining an accurate count of the homeless. In Ohio, two-thirds of the state is rural, undeveloped land, much of it heavily forested, mountainous, and accessible only on foot or by means of rough terrain vehicles. It is in these areas where some homeless people live. These include hermits who live in caves, culverts, or lean-tos; mountain people who have had a bad year in a kind of hunting/gathering society; miners who have been laid off; homeless people who prefer the woods to the street; and others who have exiled themselves. These homeless people are, in many ways, indistinguishable from the mountain or rural people who are poor but not homeless.

Nearly all of these people, the homeless and others alike, appear to have two things in common: they are heavily armed; and they do not like strangers. In setting up the study, interviews with local sheriffs and other key informants unanimously indicated that there existed every likelihood that an interviewer would have the tires on his or her car shot out and in some cases might be a target.

A county public health official helped the researchers contact some of these people. Without the help of this person—who knew most of the backwoods and had earned the respect and trust of these homeless through numerous confrontations—many of the rural homeless in Ohio would not have been reached.

The Poor versus the Homeless

It is often impossible to distinguish homeless people from other poor people. The young man sleeping off a binge on skid row may spend the night on the street, or he may have sufficient resources to rent a room in an SRO hotel. The elderly ''bag lady'' may live in an abandoned building or in a half-way house for deinstitutionalized psychiatric patients. People wandering about the city in rags may be pensioners who are poor and have nothing else to do, or be homeless.

Mobility

The nature of homelessness requires frequent, sometimes daily, relocation. Transients may migrate to the southern states during the winter months while preferring northern states in summer (see Chapter 3). A homeless person wanted by the police may find it necessary to sleep in a different location each night. Most shelters limit the number of consecutive nights a person may remain.

One of the Ohio study interviewers encountered the same homeless people first in Marietta and later in Steubenville and Youngstown. She established that they were working their way up the Ohio River and on to Cleveland. Another researcher discovered that, on the same day, a particular group of homeless men could be found at various times in a shelter, sleeping on park benches, and waiting in a bread line. In Washington, D.C., a shelter operator addressed the problem of counting that city's mobile and often elusive homeless: "There are a lot of hidden homeless who are sleeping in buildings, doubling up on a bed and sleeping in shifts, and it's hard to gauge how many there are" (Harris and Mintz 1985).

Defying Expectations

Just when researchers believe they understand the homeless, new evidence casts doubt on their ability to generalize. In many large cities, for example, conventional wisdom suggests that homeless people are more likely to seek food and shelter from churches, jails, shelters, or missions during the harsh winter months. But, some communities report little winter-to-summer fluctuation in the use of these programs or report peak demand in non-winter months.

Multiple Causation

If people became homeless for a very limited number of reasons, it might be easier to find them. If most were former mental patients, for instance, researchers might track specific cases as they moved through and out of that system; but homelessness occurs in various ways and, it seems, in every quarter. This diversity of causation makes it still more difficult to produce reliable numbers (see Chapter 4).

Given the unreliability of available methods for directly counting homeless people, observers have been forced, except in localized instances, to settle for rough estimation based on expert consensus. Even though nearly all those concerned agree that measurement is problematic, this does not stop the controversy over numbers either nationally or locally.

Many researchers have attempted to estimate numbers of homeless people in individual cities and states (U.S. General Accounting Office 1985, 59–88). Only one scientific study has been undertaken for the nation as a whole.

Studies

State/Local Studies

Many local studies have focused on that portion of the homeless population sleeping in public and private shelters and missions on a given night (cf. Human Resources Department 1982, 1983). Others have included in their counts homeless people who have been provided vouchers from welfare departments to spend several nights in an SRO or cheap hotel (cf. Robertson, Ropers, Boyers, 1984). A few have attempted counts of the street population (cf. Consortium for the Homeless 1983; Winograd 1982; Boston Emergency Shelter Commission 1983). No studies identified by the authors scientifically estimated the numbers who had been forced to move in with friends or relatives because they had lost their homes, although the 1980 census, which includes a count of unrelated families living in the same household (i.e., "doubled up"), has been used to estimate their numbers (cf. New York Department of Social Services 1984).

Local studies of the homeless, looked at collectively, suffer from several shortcomings. Because most focus only on shelter/mission clientele, people who are either lacking shelter or in other temporary lodgings remain uncounted. When homeless people, especially those outside the shelter/mission environment, are counted, the methods used encounter all of the problems in identifying and counting homeless previous noted. Unfortunately, many of these studies were conducted by those not professionally trained in social science research methods; with the result that they are not scientifically sound. Few studies of which we are aware have received the care in design and rigor of execution that are called for, given the difficulty of the research problem.

Because no agreement exists on how to define homelessness, even the more reliable studies lack comparability with one another. This makes it hard to establish where rates of homelessness are higher and whether numbers or composition are changing over time. Nearly all of the studies of which we are aware concentrate on urbanized areas. Homelessness in rural areas and small towns has been virtually ignored, except in the HUD (U.S. Department of Housing and Urban Development 1984) and Ohio (Ohio Department of Mental Health 1985) studies.

Statewide studies of the homeless are less numerous than local studies. The state of New York (see New York Department of Social Services 1984) has conducted one of the best statewide homeless studies. This report combined local studies of shelters and street people, census data, key informant surveys, and other sources in deriving a statewide estimate. Emergency shelter operators throughout California supplied estimates of the numbers of homeless in their areas for that state's study. These numbers were then aggregated to produce a statewide estimate, using the lowest number wherever a range of local estimates was available (California Department of Housing and Community Development 1985).

As nearly all of the statewide studies are quick to point out, their efforts at estimation suffer from the same shortcomings plaguing local studies. In addition, the statewide studies may introduce error when they extrapolate to areas of the state for which little or no data are available.

Estimates of the numbers of homeless, then, are barely adequate for some communities, and completely inadequate in nearly all cases at the state level.

The HUD Study

HUD's systematic effort to establish the extent of homelessness has highlighted the difficulty of this task. Critics have attacked the HUD estimates on a variety of methodological grounds (U.S. Congress 1985). Subsequent studies by the Federal Emergency Management Agency (FEMA) and the General Accounting Office (GAO) carefully avoided either confirming the HUD numbers or attempting to improve on HUD's estimates (U.S. GAO 1985). The HUD study, therefore, remains the only government attempt to determine the national scale of homelessness; and its methods and results thus deserve a brief accounting.

HUD used four independent methods of arriving at a national estimate. Each of these had acknowledged shortcomings. All use local estimates for a sample or metropolitan areas as a basis for estimating the homeless population in other metropolitan areas and in rural areas. Together, the four methods produce a range of national estimates.

The highest national estimate was obtained by combining the highest published estimates of the number of homeless in 37 localities. These were summed and then divided by the combined total population of those metropolitan areas to obtain a rate, which proved to be 25 homeless persons for every 10,000 people.[2] A straight extrapolation of this rate to the entire nation yielded a figure of 586,000 homeless. HUD researchers did not attempt to evaluate the methods underlying these local estimates; some may be based on partial counts or counts for only part of a metropolitan area. Nevertheless, this number is likely to be high for three reasons: (1) it relies on the highest published estimation for any area where more than one estimate was found; (2) it assumes that the rate of homelessness is as high in (generally small) metropolitan areas where no published estimates were obtained and in rural areas as in areas with published estimates; and (3) some of the local estimates are based on a broader definition of homelessness than HUD's or include all of those homeless at any time during a given year rather than at a point in time.

HUD's second approach to obtaining a national estimate was to conduct over 500 telephone interviews with local observers in a sample of 60 metropolitan areas. Three to five estimates were obtained for the smaller metropolitan areas and eight to twelve in the largest areas. In larger metropolitan areas, interviewers obtained separate estimates for the central city and surrounding counties. The more reliable estimates (as judged by the interviewers) were combined to calculate separate estimates of the numbers of homeless in each of the sampled metropolitan areas. Rates of homelessness were generally higher, relative to total population, in large and medium-sized areas than in small (under 250,000 population) metropolitan areas. The average rate of homelessness in small metropolitan areas was used as an estimate of the rate in nonmetropolitan areas to derive an estimate of the number of rural homeless. All estimates were then used to project a national figure, which was 254,000 homeless.

The third approach used by HUD was to survey a representative sample of emergency shelter operators in the same 60 metropolitan areas. Each was asked to estimate the number of homeless in the metropolitan area. In places where more than one shelter was sampled, the separate estimates were averaged. Then, in a fashion similar to that used in the second method, these estimates were extrapolated to a national figure. This estimate was 353,000 homeless.

Finally, HUD combined reports from the shelter survey on actual shelter occupancy with estimates of the numbers of homeless "on the streets" to obtain a fourth set of estimates. For the latter group of homeless (i.e., those outside the shelters), HUD used two independent methods of obtaining an estimate. First, "casual counts" of homeless persons at places such as bus and train stations, employment offices, and street corners, conducted in some metropolitan areas for the 1980 U.S. census, were adjusted to obtain a national estimate of 198,000. Second, the only three local studies known to have counted homeless "on the street" were used to calculate a ratio of this population to those in the shelters. Projected to the nation, this yielded an estimate of 123,000. The two estimates of the "street" population were then combined with the more reliable number of 69,000 homeless in emergency shelters obtained from the shelter survey to produce alternative national estimates of 192,000 and 267,000 homeless. Results of the four methods are shown in Table 2.1.

Recognizing the weaknesses of each method, HUD's researchers concluded that the "most reliable range" estimate, as of January 1984, was between 250,000 and 350,000 homeless people throughout the nation. It is possible that this estimate is low. HUD made no attempt at a direct count. The fourth method does use actual counts as the basis for its projections, but the other three essentially combine the opinions of informed local observers. If these observers tended to be low in their estimates, then this bias would be reflected in the overall ex-

TABLE 2.1.   HUD Estimates of the number of U.S. homeless in January 1984

Method	Estimate
Highest published estimates from local studies	586,000
Estimates from 500 key informant interviews from 60 metropolitan areas	254,000
Survey of 184 shelter operators in 60 metropolitan areas	353,000
Shelter population and street count	192,000–267,000
Most reliable range	250,000–350,000

Source: HUD. *A Report to the Secretary on the Homeless and Emergency Shelters* (Washington, D.C.: May 1984), pp. 8–21.

trapolation. Most observers might estimate low, for instance, if many homeless persons managed to conceal their presence in the community or were indistinguishable from other people. On the other hand, it is possible that observers tend to be high in their estimates, since many are sympathetic to the suffering of this group as demonstrated by their work with the homeless or their involvement in efforts to address the problem locally. They might therefore have reason to overstate the extent of homelessness. In fact, there is no way to know whether local observers tended to estimate high or low.

Whatever the limits of HUD's methodology, its numbers do result from a systematic aggregation of the best available local estimates and, therefore, constitute by far the most credible information on the extent of homelessness nationally. This has not prevented some from attacking the report's methods and motives, or caused the press to stop citing the far higher figure of two million. Oddly, though, HUD's estimates using its second method, for metropolitan areas where Mitch Snyder's group also has provided estimates, are higher than Snyder's in seven of ten cases. In fact, there are virtually no local estimates that suggest a rate of homelessness as high as one percent of the population, which is the national rate equivalent to Snyder's national estimate (Kondratas 1985b). HUD's numbers thus have greater credibility than the alternative unscientific estimates so frequently cited by the media.

To some extent, the debate over numbers has taken on the aspect of a phony war. Both sides in the debate agree that even the lowest estimates suggest a problem of disturbing magnitude calling for government action. Both sides agree that the numbers have been rising, and rapidly, since 1980. It is also important to note that, given the rate at which a portion of the U.S. homeless population turns over, a count of all those homeless within a relatively brief period such as a year would be much higher than the HUD point-in-time estimate. In Ohio, the average duration of a spell of homelessness is less than six months. HUD's review of seven local studies addressing duration and its own shelter survey both indicated that a large minority of the homeless have been in that condition for no more than a few months. HUD researchers also concluded that "a large minority are 'episodically' or occasionally homeless" (U.S. Department of HUD 1984, 30). Therefore, the number of people homeless for at least a portion of the year could be several times the number homeless at a single time.[3]

Whatever the number of homeless, there is strong evidence that the number has increased, and rapidly, within the last decade. This evidence comes from local studies throughout the country and from two national sources, the HUD study and reports by the U.S. Conference of Mayors (1984, 1986; see also Freeman and Hall, 1986). HUD asked local experts in 60 metropolitan areas, in the winter of 1983–84, whether the numbers of homeless were increasing or not, and if so, by how much. The modal response was an increase of about 10 percent a year (U.S. Dept. of HUD 1984, 16). At about the same time, the U.S. Conference of Mayors surveyed 83 cities and found an average annual rate of increase of 38 percent. In

1985, a similar survey of 25 cities found an average rate of increase of 25 percent (Waxman and Reyes 1986). However, reliable rates of increase require reliable and fairly precise baseline figures or numbers; these are simply lacking in most communities. Therefore, we cannot be sure that the numbers of homeless continue to grow or state with certainty the rate of increase for a given period of time or whether this rate is rising or falling.

The most reliable numbers regarding rates of change are those recording changes in shelter populations. For instance, a study by the Human Resources Administration of New York (1984) showed that the average nightly census of single adult shelter users during the month of January 1980 was 2,023; while in January 1985, this number had grown to 7,650.

While the available estimates suggest a rapid rate of increase in the homeless population, they could also represent in part a shift of the population from privately operated SRO hotels and other transient facilities to the public shelters as well as more effective methods of outreach, which would draw a higher proportion of people from the streets or from temporary accommodations with friends or relatives into the shelters. We simply do not have enough information to establish the true rate of increase of the homeless population either nationally or in most localities.

REGIONAL DISTRIBUTION

The HUD study, by employing an identical methodology for the entire country, allows comparisons among regions and across cities of different sizes.

The rate of homelessness differs across the four regions of the United States (Table 2.2). The West accounts for almost one-third of the homeless in the United States, although only one-fifth of the population reside there. This pattern may surprise some who believe that because of mass unemployment, tight labor markets, and declining housing stock for the poor, the Northeast and North-Central regions should have higher rates of homelessness than elsewhere.

The ratio of homeless population to total population is higher, on average, in larger metropolitan areas than in smaller ones. HUD found that there were 13 homeless people (by its definition) per 10,000 population in metropolitan areas of over one million people; 12 per 10,000 in areas of 250,000 to one million population; and just 6.5 per 10,000 in metropolitan areas of fewer than 250,000 population. According to HUD's compilation of reliable local estimates and other, unpublished sources, the ten metropolitan areas with the largest populations of homeless people in January 1984 are as shown in Table 2.3.

However, if the scale of homelessness is measured as a ratio, then the ten metropolitan areas (of 70 for which relatively reliable estimates could be obtained) with the largest numbers of homeless relative to their populations are as shown in Table 2.4.

TABLE 2.2. Numbers of homeless by census region for metropolitan areas of 50,000+, January 1984

Region	Number	Percentage of total homeless	Percentage of 1980 population
South	50,000	24	33
North-Central	45,400	22	26
Northeast	49,500	24	22
West	65,500	32	19
Totals	210,400	102*	100

Source: U.S. Dept. of HUD 1984, 20.
*Does not add to 100 percent due to rounding.

TABLE 2.3. Metropolitan areas with the largest homeless populations

Metropolitan area	Estimated number of homeless
Los Angeles	31,300–33,800
New York	28,000–30,000
Chicago	19,400–20,300
San Francisco	7,700–8,800
Detroit	7,200–7,800
Houston	5,200–7,500
Miami	5,100–6,800
Washington, D.C.	3,000–6,400
Philadelphia	2,200–5,000
Seattle	3,100–3,250

Source: U.S. Dept. of HUD 1984; also, unpublished data for some areas.

TABLE 2.4. Estimated rates of homelessness in ten metropolitan areas

Metropolitan area	Estimated rate of homelessness (per 10,000 population)
Tucson	61
El Paso	59
Worcester, MA	47
Los Angeles	40
New Orleans	34
Honolulu	33
New York	26
Las Vegas	26
Chicago	25
San Jose	25

Source: U.S. Dept. of HUD 1984; also, unpublished data for some areas.

Statistical analysis of the relationship between metropolitan area characteristics and the rate of homelessness reveals that the scale of the problem is greater not only in larger areas but in rapidly growing areas.[4] The same analysis indicates that, contrary to expectations, there is no connection between climate and the rate of homelessness, once population growth is taken into account. In other words, homeless people are concentrated in areas of expanding population and economic opportunity, many of which are in Sun Belt states; but the statistical patterns suggest that it is growth, not weather, that is associated with the higher rate of homelessness. Possibly, homeless people are drawn to growing areas by the greater economic opportunity they offer. Perhaps, also, the higher rate of development in these areas displaces more people from their homes due to the destruction of marginal housing or rapid increases in rents.

It is surprising to find that the rate of homelessness is not associated with two indicators of local housing conditions—rent levels and rental vacancy rates. In areas where rents are higher than average and where rental vacancy rates are low, it is reasonable to expect that more low-income households will have difficulty finding affordable apartments. However, when other influences are considered, there is no independent statistical relationship between the ratio of homeless population to total population and either indicator of housing market conditions.

This analysis also suggests that there are many influences on the rate of homelessness that are not so easily measured. These may include historical influences such as the presence of a ''skid row'' area where homeless people are tolerated and have access to shelter and other services. It may also include features of a state's welfare system or its housing market that are not captured by readily available statistics. Here is still another set of questions for which better information and additional analysis are needed before satisfactory answers can be given.

A PORTRAIT OF THE HOMELESS

The issues of numbers, rates, and geographic distribution aside, it is now possible using data from the Ohio survey to see more clearly who the homeless are. The Ohio survey is the first to cover the homeless population of an entire state (urban and rural areas included), and it defines homelessness to include not just those in emergency shelters or without conventional shelter but also those, in temporary accommodations such as SRO hotels or doubling with family or friends, who consider themselves homeless. This set of nearly 1,000 interviews, although limited to one state, thus constitutes a considerable advance over previous surveys conducted in a single city, many of them limited to the population of one or a few shelters. Moreover, as will be shown below, the demographics of Ohio's homeless population mirror those of the entire nation.

Degrees of Deprivation

To explore distinctions within the homeless population, it is useful to divide the entire group along dimensions of time and place of central importance in understanding that population. If homelessness is a form of severe deprivation, then the severity of that deprivation is likely to vary with the length of time a person has been homeless. In Ohio, 40 percent of the homeless population had been without regular accommodation for less than 30 days when interviewed. At the other extreme, 16 percent had been homeless for two years or longer and 24 percent for at least one year. Not only does the hardship of having no home increase with the passage of time; those who are homeless longer have characteristics and problems different from those recently made homeless. With regard to the dimension of place, the severity of deprivation is greater for those who live without shelter or in makeshift accommodations they arrange for themselves than for those in emergency shelters. The least degree of deprivation may be experienced by those who have turned to family or friends or who have enough money to pay for short-term accommodations. Of the Ohio sample, 15 percent are people "on the street" (i.e., without any form of conventional shelter), 60 percent are in emergency shelters, and 25 percent are in other temporary accommodations.[5]

The distribution of the Ohio sample on these two dimensions is shown in Table 2.5. Those at the lower left have suffered the greatest deprivation, as mea-

TABLE 2.5. Distribution of the Ohio sample by source of shelter and duration of homelessness

	Source of shelter			
Duration	No shelter	Emergency shelter	Other temporary	Totals (n)
Less than 30 days	6.5 (61)	21.5 (203)	11.3 (107)	39.3 (371)
31 days to 1 year	4.5 (42)	20.5 (193)	9.0 (85)	33.9 (320)
More than 1 year	3.1 (29)	14.6 (138)	4.0 (38)	21.7 (205)
No answer	0.7 (7)	3.0 (28)	1.3 (12)	5.0 (47)
Totals (n)	14.7 (139)	59.6 (562)	25.7 (242)	100.0 (943)

Figures are percentages; figures in parentheses are size of sample.
Source: Ohio Deparment of Mental Health 1985.

sured by these two characteristics; those at the upper right have suffered the least deprivation.

Using this matrix, we can look at the demographic characteristics of Ohio's homeless population and how these vary with two important indicators of deprivation. Images of the homeless as aging vagrants or more youthful drifters dominated the public's perceptions during the early part of this century. More recently, vague conceptions of a "new homelessness" affecting individuals and families have added complexity to the commonly held picture. However, the view that emerges from the Ohio survey is even more complex, showing a population highly varied in its demographic characteristics and probably in less obvious ways as well.

Age

More than one-half of Ohio's adult homeless population is under 40, and 35 percent are between the ages of 18 and 29. At the other extreme, 7 percent are over 60 years old. The average age is 33 years. However, those who have been homeless for more than one year are significantly older (36 years), on average, than other homeless (31 years) (Table 2.6). Homeless people on the streets (36 years) or in emergency shelters (34 years) tend to be older than those living temporarily in other accommodations (28 years). People who are on the streets and have been homeless more than one year are likely to be much older than

TABLE 2.6. Average age (years) by source of shelter and duration of homelessness

	Source of shelter			
Duration	No shelter	Emergency shelter	Other temporary	Totals (n)
Less than 30 days	34 (67)	33 (229)	27 (118)	31 (414)
31 days to 1 year	33 (36)	34 (161)	27 (72)	32 (269)
More than 1 year	43 (34)	37 (165)	31 (50)	36 (249)
Totals (n)	36 (137)	34 (555)	28 (240)	33 (932)

Figures are percentages; figures in parentheses are sample size.
Source: Ohio Department of Mental Health 1985.

those in temporary accommodations other than shelters and have been homeless for less than 30 days. In short, those who are most deprived also tend to be older.

Sex

The traditional image of the homeless person is male. However, in Ohio as elsewhere, the proportion of female homeless appears to have increased in recent years. Nineteen percent of those interviewed were women (Table 2.7). Women are less likely than men to have been homeless for a long time (only 10 percent of those homeless for more than one year are women), but this may partly reflect the fact that their proportion among the homeless has only recently increased. Women are also much less likely to live on the streets or in shelters, but are much more likely to live in other temporary accommodations. Overall, women appear to experience homelessness for shorter periods of time and tend to find or choose better accommodations than men.

Race

In Ohio, today, blacks make up nearly one-third of the homeless. Compared to others, Blacks tend to be homeless for a shorter time and, possibly for this reason, have not been forced to or chosen to live on the streets as often as whites (Table 2.8).

TABLE 2.7. Percentage female by source of shelter and duration of homelessness

Duration	Source of shelter			
	No shelter	Emergency shelter	Other temporary	Totals (n)
Less than 30 days	11.8 (68)	22.9 (231)	25.2 (119)	21.8 (418)
31 days to 1 year	18.9 (37)	16.7 (162)	41.7 (72)	23.6 (271)
More than 1 year	0.0 (34)	9.5 (169)	17.7 (51)	9.8 (254)
Totals (n)	10.8 (139)	17.1 (562)	28.5 (242)	19.1 (943)

Figures in parentheses are sample sizes.
Source: Ohio Department of Mental Health 1985.

TABLE 2.8. Percentage of Blacks by source of shelter and duration of homelessness

Duration	Source of shelter			
	No shelter	Emergency shelter	Other temporary	Totals (n)
Less than 30 days	32.4 (68)	41.4 (227)	23.8 (119)	37.4 (414)
31 days to 1 year	18.9 (37)	25.5 (161)	23.9 (71)	24.2 (269)
More than 1 year	0.0 (34)	26.8 (161)	27.5 (71)	25.8 (269)
Totals (n)	25.4 (138)	32.4 (556)	29.0 (241)	30.5 (935)

Figures in parentheses are sample sizes.
Source: Ohio Department of Mental Health 1985.

Education

It is widely believed that, in the past, most homeless people were poorly educated but that, in harder economic times, well-educated people are more likely to be made homeless. In Ohio, 45 percent of the homeless possess a high school diploma. Of these, nearly one-half have either started or finished college-level work. Those staying in shelters or other temporary lodgings and homeless for short periods (less than 30 days) average slightly higher levels of education than others who are more deprived; but the differences across the categories are small and not consistent in direction (Table 2.9).

Marital and Family Status

Fewer than ten percent of the Ohio homeless are currently married, and another two percent are living with someone of the other sex. However, 25 percent are divorced, 14 percent are separated, and five percent are widows or widowers. The remaining 45 percent have never married—a rather high proportion considering that only 25 percent of all adults in Ohio have never been married.

Because of the manner in which the Ohio survey was conducted, there is no information available for analysis on the numbers of children the homeless have, either living with them or living elsewhere. However, a reliable estimate placed the number of intact families (i.e., units of at least one parent and one

TABLE 2.9. Percentage with at least a high school diploma by source of shelter and duration of homelessness

| Duration | No shelter | Source of shelter | | Totals (n) |
		Emergency shelter	Other temporary	
Less than 30 days	44.8 (67)	51.5 (229)	50.4 (119)	50.1 (415)
31 days 1 year	27.0 (37)	44.4 (162)	35.2 (71)	39.6 (270)
More than 1 year	44.1 (34)	40.8 (169)	46.9 (49)	42.5 (252)
Totals (n)	39.9 (138)	46.3 (560)	45.2 (239)	45.0 (937)

Figures in parentheses are sample sizes.
Source: Ohio Deparment of Mental Health 1985.

child) homeless in the Cleveland metropolitan area in late 1985 at between 30 and 50 on a given night.[6] Given the estimated numbers of homeless adults in the Cleveland area, this suggests that about 10 percent of the adult homeless in that part of the state are accompanied by their children.

Table 2.10 summarizes the demographic characteristics of the Ohio sample.

OHIO AND THE NATION

The demographic profile of the nation's homeless presented in HUD's report in most respects resembles that found in Ohio. The department's national survey of shelter operators and its average of 20 local studies produced virtually identical numbers: two-thirds single men, about one in seven single women, and about one in five members of intact families. If we assume that over 80 percent of the families are headed by a woman with, on average, two children then the proportions of adult homeless nationally divide between the two sexes in roughly the same proportion as the Ohio sample (i.e., over three-fourths are males).

HUD found the median age of the adult homeless nationally to be between the late twenties to mid-thirties, with the average being 34. HUD also estimated that 6 percent were over 60 and 10 to 15 percent were over 50. The age distribution for the Ohio sample is similar: a median age in the early thirties, with

TABLE 2.10. Selected demographics for the Ohio homeless sample

Demographic Characteristic	Percentage of sample
Sex	
Male	81.0
Female	19.0
Race	
White	65.9
Minority	34.1
Blacks	30.5
Age	
18–29	35.2
30–39	27.9
40–49	17.0
50–59	13.4
60+	6.5
Education	
1–8 years	17.3
9–11 years	37.7
High school	30.8
Some college	14.2
Marital status	
Married	9.1
Separated	14.1
Widowed	4.5
Divorced	25.0
Living together	2.2
Never married	45.0

Source: Ohio Department of Mental Health 1985.

7 percent over 60 and a somewhat higher proportion than HUD's national estimate, nearly 20 percent, over 50.

HUD estimated that 44 percent of the homeless in shelters are minorities. Since only 20 percent of the U.S. population is Black, Hispanic, or other minorities, this suggests that this group is overrepresented among the homeless as they are among the poor generally. In Ohio, 34 percent of the homeless interviewed were minority, compared to 10 percent of the state's population. The current overrepresentation of minorities among the homeless is believed by many to represent a significant change from previous decades, but there is probably no way to confirm this or other supposed shifts in the demographics of homelessness.

CONCLUSION

This chapter has reviewed the debate over numbers and noted the various ways that homelessness can be defined, its scale measured, and its components divided into degrees of deprivation and demographic categories. The U.S. homeless population of the 1980s is demographically diverse, probably much more so than in preceding decades. The information on employment status and income presented in the next chapter, and the exploration of how people become homeless in Chapter 4, of psychological status in Chapter 5, and of the varied service needs of the homeless in Chapter 6 will add depth to the picture presented here and will reinforce the conclusion that this is a diverse group, although it is caught up in common circumstances.

NOTES

1. The definition chosen also will affect estimates of the extent to which the numbers of homeless have changed over time. For example, if the narrower place definition is used, then the substitution of emergency shelters for SROs and flophouses, which has occurred in many cities over the last decade, would increase the numbers counted as homeless in those cities. If the broader definition were used, the substitution of shelters for these other temporary residences would not increase the homeless count.

2. Considerable controversy has surrounded HUD's selection of the Rand McNally Area (RMA) rather than the commonly used Standard Metropolitan Statistical Area (SMSA) that was used, through 1980, by the U.S. Bureau of the Census to define metropolitan areas. The RMA has been used for many years, mainly for commercial purposes. In all but a few cases, it is less extensive geographically than the SMSA, because it excludes the lightly populated rural fringe areas of counties included in SMSA. However, for the three largest metropolitan areas, the RMA is considerably *more* extensive than the SMSA. Also, in these three areas, critics of the HUD study noted that no estimates were obtained for counties outside the SMSA but included in the RMA. This apparent error may have lowered HUD's national estimate by a few percent.

3. One well-informed observer gives these two estimates for numbers of homeless in the Cleveland, Ohio metropolitan area: (1) "300 to 400 on a given night" and (2) "5,000 over the course of a year."

4. This discussion is based on a multiple regression analysis in which five independent variables (population; population growth from 1970 to 1982; annual degree-days of heating; 1983 rental vacancy rate; and average rent for a modest standard rental unit) were regresssed against the estimated 1983–84 rate of homelessness for 71 metropolitan areas. Only the first two variables were found to be significantly related to the rate of homelessness. Together, they explain only 15 percent of the variation in rates across metropolitan areas.

5. Because of the sampling procedure, it was impossible to establish the correct proportional representation between levels of homelessness (street, shelter, and other temporary). The different sampling rates for these three components of the homeless population are an additional reason why separate demographics are presented here for each group and why, in subsequent chapters, any differences related to this categorization are noted. There are widely differing local estimates of the ratio between numbers in shelters and those on the street or in other exposed locations. These range from nearly three unsheltered for every one sheltered (Phoenix; U.S. Dept. of HUD 1984) to one unsheltered for every 25 sheltered (Nashville, in winter; Wiegand 1985).

6. Conversation with Larry Kameya, Cleveland United Way, December 1985.

—— 3 ——

SURVIVING

We're about down and out. . .the only good thing about it. . .is that there's not much farther we can go.[1]

Unemployed man, 1935

Most Americans, beneficiaries of the greatest accumulation of wealth ever by one people, can scarcely imagine survival without a home. Even those living in extreme poverty may find it difficult to understand subsistence outside the ghetto tenement or rural tarpaper shack. Yet, incomprehensibly, hundreds of thousands of Americans cope from day to day with no permanent or reliable shelter. This chapter describes how the homeless make ends meet.

To understand homeless people, and to assist them through public and private programs and initiatives, we must first know how they meet two basic needs: sleeping and eating. What sleeping accommodations and food sources are available to the homeless? Why are some preferred to others? How often and why do the homeless move from one sleeping location to another? How adequate are the shelter and food typically available to the homeless? Who provides them with necessities?

In most households, life is organized around work; having a job or income is of paramount importance. Therefore, most people invest in preparing for work through education. When out of work, they actively search for work, and are willing to accept a suitable job when it is offered. To what extent do the ranks of the homeless include those who cannot find work, do not choose to work, would be undesirable at work, or are so debilitated that working is impossible? Of those who have worked, what kinds of jobs were held and why were those jobs lost? If not working, where do homeless people get the money to live on? What kinds of things do homeless people spend their money on?

Homelessness implies that a person has few resources of his/her own and must depend on public or private aid. In addition to shelter and food, what other public or private services do the homeless seek? How often do they use the services available to them? How much do the homeless rely on friends and relatives to get by?

UNDERSTANDING THE HOMELESS AND THEIR ENVIRONMENT

To understand how the homeless make ends meet, we will examine different types of homeless people, their environment, and the array of social services and social networks that support them. For this purpose, it is useful to divide the population into two categories: the long-term and recently homeless (e.g., Lamb 1982c, 465; Baxter and Hopper 1982, 393). The long-term homeless include some for whom homelessness has become a way of life, either by choice or circumstance. Higher proportions of this group suffer severe psychological disorders, cannot function because of alcohol or drug abuse, are severely physically disabled, or simply prefer the life of a transient. They are more often unable to cope with personal crises or problems, to fit well within social or family relationships, or to take responsibility for themselves or others (see Lamb 1982c).

The inner city—the traditional habitat of the down and out—where tolerance and indifference are the norms, offering almost complete anonymity, as well as shelters and services specifically for this group, is often more attractive to these homeless than available alternatives. Some of the long-term homeless have been pressured into the more accommodating habitat of the inner city by police or merchants in other locales. Police in Santa Cruz, California, where some call the homeless "trolls," were asked not to wear t-shirts emblazoned with a "Troll Buster" logo when off duty. A Fort Lauderdale city commissioner suggested placing rat poison in trash dumpsters to rid the area of menacing homeless people (Leo 1985). Merchants in Youngstown, Ohio, demanded that the city council consider an ordinance making it illegal to search trash dumpsters for food. A priest in Dallas who provides services to the poor reports that homeless "people who camp at the outskirts of the city endure 'tremendous abuse by young punks who prey on them and beat them, sometimes very sadistically' " (Leo 1985, 68). Such actions force both the long-term and newly homeless into the relatively friendlier environment of the big city, and within it usually into a bounded and commonly recognized "homeless habitat."

The homeless habitat goes by different names in different cities. The Bowery in New York City, the Tenderloin District in San Francisco, and the original "Skid Row" in Seattle are some of the best known; but every large city has such a zone. Most of the long-term homeless are aware of these zones and move into them. Until recently, there has been an unwritten law that homeless people would be tolerated as long as they remained in the homeless habitat—keeping the homeless out of sight and out of mind. However, in the 1980s, homeless people became more numerous within the traditional zones; and also turned up in significant numbers outside the zones—in smaller cities and towns, and, increasingly, in suburban areas (Kerr 1985). In Youngstown, Ohio, for example, church congregations in middle- and working-class neighborhoods were shocked, beginning in 1984, to see homeless people regularly attending social functions where free meals or refreshments were being served. The breakdown of the traditional bounded areas in cities is one reason for increased public awareness of the homeless problem (see also the box below).

The homeless habitat and the formal system that provides them with basic services have evolved together over time. This system provides minimal food, shelter, and clothing to meet basic needs of homeless people. Occasionally, the system offers subsistence wages or subsidies for day labor, allowing homeless people to purchase necessities or extras: drink, drugs, temporary lodging, sex, clothing, or toiletries. The system may also provide counseling, basic and emergency health care, religious instruction, and companionship; but these services do not appear nearly as important to most homeless as food and shelter. Although established primarily to serve the long-term homeless, this system also serves those recently made homeless and, in many cities, increasing numbers of homeless women and children. The homeless habitat and the patchwork system of shelter and social services is an arrangement convenient both for the homeless and for the rest of society.

MEETING A BASIC NEED

In December 1985, about 75 homeless people occupied most of the 101 toilets in San Francisco's city hall. Their protest was in support of a city supervisor's proposal to lease 25 high-tech portable toilets, at $12,000 a year each, and place these in areas with many pedestrians, where they could be used by the homeless as well as tourists, office workers, and shoppers. Both the homeless and store owners in the city's Tenderloin District supported the idea as an alternative to the unpleasant and unhealthy results when homeless people relieve themselves in alleys and doorways. The automatic toilets have power-assisted doors, washbasins, mirrors, and toilets that automatically cleanse themselves. Doors are programmed to spring open after 17 minutes to discourage loitering. These toilets are now common in Paris, where use costs one franc; but, since they are intended for the homeless in San Francisco, they will be free.

Source: Mark A. Stein. "Homeless People Publicize Potty Shortage." *Los Angeles Times*, December 14, 1985.

The homeless services system, as we know it today, does not deal effectively with the needs of the homeless. In some cases, it furthers the isolation of the homeless and extends their stay beyond the margins of normal society. In some communities, the rapid increase in numbers of homeless or the changing composition of the homeless population have badly strained the traditional services system.

Much of the formal human services system is geared toward the needs of the poor in general but not the homeless specifically. Simple requirements, like 30 days' residency and a permanent address make the standard public assistance programs irrelevant for some homeless people, especially the more transient. Many services are operated by private charitable organizations that impose stringent conditions: homeless recipients must stay sober, often must accept religious instruction, may be asked to say grace before meals, cannot sleep with an unmarried partner, and so on (see box below). Public organizations impose their own biases on the homeless, requiring them to fill out paperwork, participate in research, or accept diagnostic testing and counseling from professional social workers (see also, Bassuk 1984, 44). If they reject such intrusions, the homeless must return to the often dangerous environment of the city streets (see also Chapter 7).

TOLEDO POLICE LOSERS IN ATTEMPTS TO CHANGE LIFE STYLE OF "BAG LADY"

TOLEDO, Ohio (AP)—A 60-year-old woman who lives in downtown alleys and doorways is being arrested repeatedly for minor violations because police say they have to follow up on complaints about her and she refuses to give up her "bag lady" life style.

Elaine Higgins has become perhaps the most well-known homeless person in the city since she began living in the streets about 10 years ago, say police who arrested her Tuesday just six hours after she was released from jail after serving five days for a loitering conviction.

Police Chief John Mason said he has ordered officers to arrest her whenever she is seen breaking the law, because her presence and the large collection of bottles, bags, umbrellas and other possessions she carries with her are sparking citizens' complaints.

The most recent complaints have ranged from blocking sidewalks and hindering pedestrians to defecating and urinating in the street, Mason said.

Ms. Higgins has declined to be placed in an institution.

"She's very comfortable and satisfied with her life style and does not want to change it." Mason said Wednesday.

He said the recent arrests are the latest in a long-running attempt to find shelter for Ms. Higgins and satisfy downtown workers who do not want her camping outside their businesses.

The police division and several other agencies have tried unsuccessfully to get Ms. Higgins placed in an institution, but her mental condition does not qualify under an Ohio law that would let police hospitalize someone believed to be mentally ill or who could pose a risk of physical harm to themselves or others, Mason said.

In 1982, Downtown Toledo Associates, a now-disbanded business group, asked the Lucas County Probate Court to commit her to the Toledo Mental Health Center, but was told Ms. Higgins isn't a risk to anyone and cannot be committed by the court.

Police and jailers said Ms. Higgins, who does not have a lawyer, is handled separately from other prisoners because none of them wants to share a cell with her because of sanitation concerns, but otherwise she is treated like any other inmate.

In addition to her recent arrests on loitering charges, Ms. Higgins has been arrested by police at least 23 times in the last 15 years on charges of loitering, criminal trespassing, disorderly conduct, public indecency, disturbing the peace, shoplifting, intoxication, and soliciting.

She has been convicted on a number of the misdemeanor counts and fined or sentenced to jail terms from five to 30 days.

(As printed in *The Youngstown Vindicator*, September 1, 1985.)
Reprinted by permission from the Associated Press.

Under pressure from growing numbers of homeless and increasing media attention, and with growing government support, the homeless services system has rapidly expanded and, in some cases, improved. A few observers of this change (cf. Main 1983a, 1983b) have suggested that the public shelters have been made so attractive that they are luring poor people who could and have in the past found food and shelter without assistance. In this view, the attraction of free bed and board, often without restriction (e.g., a client does not have to work even though work might be available) may have changed the composition of the long-term homeless population by attracting some who find the shelters more attractive or affordable than any readily available alternative. However, there is not much evidence to support this assertion.

Those who are homeless for short periods or who have just become homeless also tend to concentrate in the urban homeless habitat, where most services for the homeless are located. Unlike the long-term homeless, the recently homeless may enter the system only once and remain within it for a relatively short time. This group may be more responsive to assistance, because they are more able to help themselves and more willing to accept help from others, including establishing their eligibility for public assistance, food stamps, and/or subsidized housing. Many of these families and individuals move through the shelter system in the course of a year, remaining only until they can establish a stable source of income and find permanent accommodations.

Many rural or small-town homeless people also make their way to the urban homeless habitat. Few rural areas and small towns have specialized services for the homeless. Although HUD's study did not provide separate estimates for rural areas, it does confirm that rates of homelessness are much lower in metropolitan areas of less than 250,000 population than in larger metropolitan areas. This is consistent with the view that big cities serve as catch basins for many people who are made homeless in nonurban areas and then exported, sometimes forcibly (see Anderson 1983, 15).

SHELTER

Most local programs to serve homeless people operate through a private mission or public shelter. However, many homeless people either lack access to or avoid the shelters. If accommodation in shelters is unavailable because of excess demand for limited space, or is inappropriate, because some of those in need require different quarters (e.g., families who cannot be accommodated in facilities designed for single adults), vouchers may be provided for a short-term stay at a cheap hotel, motel, or rooming house. Other homeless remain on the street or in makeshift shelters such as abandoned buildings or automobiles. Others, perhaps with more resources or connections to others, find temporary lodging with friends or family.

RESCUE MISSION REGULATIONS

God loves you; one way he shows his love is by giving you food, clothing, and a bed here at the Rescue Mission. If we can help in any other ways, please let us know. There is no charge *for any of this.*

Your cooperation is expected. If you don't care for our regulations, you are free to go elsewhere. Remember God Will Bless You, only as much as you let him!!!

1. *This Room is for sitting. Do not lay on the benches or on the floor.*
2. *This room is closed from 7:15–11:00 a.m. Everyone must be gone during these hours. All bags, clothing, or anything else left here, will be thrown away.*
3. *You may get your mail at this address. In exchange you must work 9 hours each week for us. If you are interested see Chaplain Larry.* NO WORK—NO MAIL!!!

4. *Check-in time is 8:00 p.m.–11:00 p.m. After 10:00 p.m. everyone must check in and go upstairs. No sitting around. The doors will be locked at 11:00 p.m. each night. No one who has been here before will be admitted after 11:00 p.m. unless prior arrangements have been made in writing with Chaplain Larry.*
5. *Everyone* must *take a shower and wear pajamas we provide.* No exceptions!!! NO SHOWER—NO BED!!!
6. *Do not bring food into the building—it attracts roaches and mice.*
7. *You will be* BARRED *from getting any help from mission if you:*
   a. *smoke inside the building*
   b. *light a smoke inside building*
   c. *bring any alcohol or illegal drugs inside the building*
   d. *destroy, deface, or steal any mission property*
   e. *verbally or physically abuse resident program man or woman, staff or client.*
8. Meals *are at* 6:45 a.m., Noon, 5:00 p.m. *Sundays:* 6:45 a.m., 1:00 p.m., 6:00 p.m. Clothing *is provided at* 8:00 a.m. *every Wednesday. Chapel Services are provided at* 7:30 p.m. *Monday through Saturday;* 2:00 p.m. *Sunday.*

Source: Rescue Mission, City of Youngstown.

It is generally assumed that increased shelter capacity would eliminate the need of many homeless to live in the street and reduce the burden on family and friends who have temporarily taken in others. However, the relationship between supply and demand for shelter space is complex (see Chapter 7). If simple lack of capacity were the problem, one would expect to find virtually all homeless people either in shelters or other temporary accommodation where space is available. Such is not the case. Several studies have noted a large number of people living on the street, even where and when shelter space is available (Baxter and Hopper 1982; U.S. Dept of HUD 1984).

Many of those on the street or in other exposed locations are there because they prefer this to other options (Baxter and Hopper 1982). The street, for some, poses a more comfortable or less threatening environment than the shelter. A person who has difficulty coping with people can sit in a doorway and not be bothered. People who behave strangely by excessively talking to themselves or by collecting string or tinfoil are left alone. No one cares or if they do care, they usually do not interfere. In some cases, individual pride may keep a person out of shelters: "I went to one [shelter] once, but there was nothing there but bums. I ain't no bum and it will never come to that. I'm a normal guy, I just ain't got a home" (Anderson 1983, 15).

Some homeless fear or are unable to tolerate the shelter environment (see Baxter and Hopper 1982, 398). And, in fact, some shelters are dirty and inhospitable. People with severe psychological disorders may scream periodically through the night. Because some homeless have not bathed recently, offensive body odors and body lice may follow in their wake. For this reason, shelters may require entering homeless to strip and bathe while their clothes are washed, an experience to which some prefer not to submit. In the shelter, a drug or alcohol abuser may vomit on his fellow boarders as he "comes down" from a chemically induced high. People who prey on the weak often assault and steal from others in the shelters. One shelter operator in New York City reports that "older men sleep gripping their shoes so they aren't stolen by the newer arrivals" (Alter 1984, 22).

Homeless who are staying temporarily in cheap hotels and motels may be no better off than those in shelters. Some of these establishments offer few amenities. Rooms are poorly heated in winter, are not air conditioned in summer, and are shared by rats and other vermin. In some, clean linen or bedding is rare; in many, noise levels are high because of their proximity to rail yards, highways, bars, or factories.

Like most shelters, cheap hotels and motels are located in poor neighborhoods. Residents of either can expect to be victimized by others who share this territory. In Los Angeles' skid row, some years ago, several homeless winos were murdered by stabbing and slashing for no apparent motive other than that they were homeless. In New York's Hell's Kitchen, in 1981, a 67-year-old homeless woman was raped and stabbed to death (Kates 1985). Because there are no statistics on the frequency with which the homeless are victims of crime, we can only speculate that their presence in dangerous neighborhoods and their obvious vulnerability put them at great risk.

Living temporarily with others may offer greater safety and better accommodations than the street, a shelter, or a SRO; but such arrangements are often unpleasant for both the permanent occupants and their guests. Often, people turn to family or friends when they lack the means or personal strength to continue living independently. Even here, the homeless person may become the victim of sexual or physical abuse by others (see case study following); or an elderly person may be required to sign over a Social Security or pension check to relatives. Again, there is no way to know the frequency with which homeless people are thus victimized.

Whatever their source of shelter on a particular night, it is by definition temporary. Homeless people must continually move in order to find better or to avoid worsening circumstances. When the Ohio homeless were asked how many different places they had stayed during the month before the interview, two-fifths indicated that they had stayed in at least three different places.

Asked where they had spent the previous night and where they planned to spend the night (see Table 3.1), 85 percent said that they would stay in the same place as they had the night before. However, even 15 percent of the homeless changing accommodations from one night to the next is obviously much higher than the rate at which other segments of the population change residence.

Constant movement of people in and out of the shelters results not only from the time limits that shelters impose on occupancy but also the changing circumstances of the homeless population. However, nearly all of those currently in an

TABLE 3.1. Where spent last night by plans for this night

| Where spent last night | Where planning to spend this night | | | | | | |
	No shelter	Car etc.	Mission/ shelter	Cheap hotel, etc.	Family/ friends	Other	Totals
No shelter	10.6	0.7	3.3	0.3	0.4	0.2	142
Car, etc.	0.4	9.1	2.2	0.4	0.5	0.4	120
Mission/shelter	0.3	0.2	31.9	0.1	0.7	0.4	304
Cheap hotel, etc.	0.0	0.2	1.1	16.5	0.1	0.0	164
Family/friends	0.3	0.4	1.2	0.1	8.4	0.2	98
Other	0.2	0.0	0.2	0.1	0.1	3.6	40
Totals	109	97	365	161	95	41	868

Source: Ohio Department of Mental Health 1985.

Ohio mission or shelter expected to spend the next night in the same or a different shelter. Of those with no shelter, about one in five expected to spend the next night in a shelter (see Table 3.1). Longer-term tracking of these patterns could be very useful in designing new approaches to reduce the need to move from better to worse accommodations or to stabilize accommodations for those who otherwise would be constantly moving. In the absence of such studies, we have here only a glimpse of the constant movement and uncertainty that characterize the homeless person's search for accommodations.

FOOD

Much of the time, securing a meal is the most pressing need for the home-less person, more immediate and urgent than the need for shelter. Having little or no money and having no place to store or prepare food forces many home-less people to focus much of their attention on where the next meal is coming from.

Although it is very likely that some homeless are undernourished, they are virtually all able to obtain food somehow. In Ohio, fewer than 3 percent of the homeless indicated that they were mostly doing without regular meals.

The soup kitchen, most often operated by local churches or by helping or-ganizations such as the Salvation Army, is probably the major source of food for the homeless. In any major U.S. city, long lines of men in tattered cloth-ing, and an occasional single woman or family group, can be seen waiting to receive meals. In Ohio, soup kitchens or similar sources are considered by more than one-half of the homeless population to be their primary source of food. An-other 10 percent reported taking meals at soup kitchens at least on some occa-sions. There are few soup kitchens or missions in rural areas. In fact, the greater prevalence of hunger in rural than in urban areas and the relative lack of feeding programs may be one reason for the concentration of the homeless in larger cities. Nearly 70 percent of the homeless in urban areas depend in some way on soup kitchens.

However, for some homeless, soup kitchens are not the main source of food. Those who show up too late to receive a meal, and those who may have difficulty coping with crowds, waiting in line, eating with strangers, or accepting the social stigma of taking a handout get their food by other means. About 17 percent of the Ohio homeless have their food given to them by others. One poor Ohio woman, over the last decade, has devoted her life to caring for homeless people. Operating out of a small house and garage in a rural area, she provides beds and home-cooked meals to homeless people who find their way to her. Her services are made possible by donations of food from neighbors and local churches. Public human services agencies have sent homeless people to her home when they were ineligible for or unwilling to accept public services. It was not unusual, in fact, for interviewers to find people with few resources of their own helping others in greater need.

Even though homeless, some people can eke out an existence by carefully planning and consuming meals in restaurants, usually of the fast-food or "greasy spoon" variety. Seven percent of those in Ohio reported that restaurants were their major source of food. Restaurants in poorer areas are often gathering places for homeless people. Some go there to obtain a meal because it is the only place they can afford. Others seek temporary shelter and comfort (air conditioning in summer, heat in winter) by buying something on the menu and remaining there much of the day or night. Still others appear to congregate with their friends in search of companionship. At several locations in Ohio, restaurant managers were observed showing respect for the needs of homeless people. In most cases, as long as they were well-behaved, the homeless were not thrown out of these establishments. In other cases, the manager provided coffee at no charge or sometimes on credit. One restaurant employed homeless people to sweep parking lots and sidewalks in exchange for food.

Some of the homeless use their scarce resources to purchase food either at food stores or from vending machines. In Ohio, 17 percent purchase food from these sources. Some take the food back to their hotel or motel and prepare it, usually illegally on a hot plate or by running warm water over the can. Others living in out-of-the-way places—under bridges, in culverts, or in tent communities—build campfires in a fashion reminiscent of hobo camps in post-World War I America. Those living in abandoned buildings often cook there as well. One fire chief expressed concern that, along with juvenile delinquents, the homeless could be a major cause of fires in vacant, condemned buildings.

Two of the least conventional ways of obtaining food—searching trash receptacles and stealing—apparently are not often used by the homeless in Ohio. About one person in 100 admitted to searching dumpsters for food; and virtually no one admitted to stealing. Because these behaviors are socially undesirable or illegal, the extent of this behavior is probably understated. It may also be that this behavior is misinterpreted on occasion. Several homeless people were seen raiding trash dumpsters on a continual basis. They were not, as it initially appeared, searching for food, but instead were collecting aluminum cans they hoped to sell at a local recycling center.

Patterns of meal taking are explained in part by an examination of the overall resources of the homeless. People in the street and in shelters tend to rely much more heavily on soup kitchens, while people with money enough to stay in SRO hotels or other cheap accommodations prefer to eat in restaurants or to buy food and prepare it. Those who resort to searching trash receptacles and stealing, even though few in number, are primarily those who live in the shelters or on the street.

WORK

Some homeless people are unable or unwilling to work. Others can work, would like jobs, and would be productive were it not for some personal crisis or disability. Some are working.

For the homeless, work is often a short-term proposition, a way to get cash for immediate needs or to move on to another town. For the homeless person, money for a bus ticket can mean the difference between going hungry in a Northern city and being with relatives in the South. A few dollars secures a place in a flophouse with a bed, a shower, and a meal for a day or so. Pocket change may enable the homeless person to splurge on a meal at a restaurant. As with most people, just having some money on hand, even if there is no immediate need to spend it, provides a small sense of comfort and security.

Other homeless pursue work opportunities as part of an effort to rebuild their lives and return to a more stable and secure living pattern. The victim of a plant closing only recently made homeless might be off the street if only a small amount of money were available to purchase tools and equipment. An older worker whose skills are no longer in demand may seek retraining in order to resume a productive work life. A worker loses his job, takes a short vacation to "get himself together," and returns to his apartment to discover he has been unlawfully evicted; with appropriate legal counsel, the worker would not be homeless. The rumor of jobs in a city far away lures an unemployed worker, only to discover the rumor was false; money to return home would eliminate homelessness for this worker.

Labor economists provide one framework with which to understand the relationship between work and homelessness. Three dimensions are typically used to characterize labor force participation: (1) "economic reward," how much financial benefit is received from work; (2) "attachment," the degree to which people want and are willing to search for and hold a job; and (3) "utilization," the extent to which groups not working are available for work.

The three dimensions can be combined into one continuum reflecting more reward, attachment, and utilization on one end and less reward, detachment, and nonutilization on the other. On one end of the continuum are those who have difficulty finding or keeping jobs, are unskilled or inexperienced, have obligations (such as family responsibilities) that prevent them from taking available jobs, are disabled or in poor health, are poor, or just do not want to work. People so classified are considered to be in the labor reserve and are often referred to as the "secondary labor force," "subemployed," "difficult to employ," or "not in the labor force." Toward the other extreme are those who have always worked at full-time jobs, earn decent salaries, enjoy an acceptable quality of life, are skilled or easily trainable, and when unemployed, have a high probability of becoming reemployed. People at this end of the continuum are considered to be the core or "primary labor force."

Based on their incomes and other attributes, one would expect the homeless population to fall largely on the labor reserve end of the combined labor force continuum. Some will never have worked, and those who have held jobs will either have had a great deal of difficulty doing so or will have worked at unskilled menial labor. Those in the core labor force, composed of those with experience and good work records and of those who have been adequately educated in high school or college to accept a job, would be far less likely to become homeless simply because they have the means to pay for housing.

To the extent that homeless people are in the labor reserve, then, we would expect they will either have little work experience or have worked intermittently. In Ohio, 84 percent of the homeless have had some work experience. At least in the past, they have been capable of working. However, few of these are currently working, even at part-time jobs. Only 28 percent said, when interviewed, that they had worked within the last month (but see box below).

HOMELESS ENTREPRENEURS

The long-term homeless are sometimes depicted as either unable or unwilling to work. Those who do hold jobs often perform manual work on a temporary basis. However, Ohio researchers encountered entrepreneurs among one group of homeless people living in an abandoned motel in a rural area. Deciding to start their own business, they assembled old clothing, food, and other items of little use to most people but valuable to the homeless. As other homeless people passing through the area sought shelter in the old motel, these entrepreneurs would sell them goods. The researchers were unable to determine how much profit was made on the venture, but business was difficult because police periodically evicted these businesspeople.

Studies of labor force participation consistently show that the longer one is out of the labor force, the less likely one is to return (Job 1979). The freedom or leisure of not working, even if it involves living on the street, in a shelter, or with friends, may be more attractive to some than the demands of work; in other cases, a long period without income from employment may affect attitudes, behavior, appearance, or health in ways that make return to work less and less likely. In Ohio, a majority (62 percent) of the homeless who had ever worked had not worked within the last two years. This suggests that they are now only weakly attached to the labor force. On the other hand, slightly over one-half of the Ohio homeless continue to show some interest in working. Most of these say that they are unemployed because they cannot find a job (47 percent); only a few say they are not now looking but plan to look for work (5 percent) or that they do not know where to look (1 percent).

The remainder of the Ohio homeless population cannot or will not work, indicating little or no attachment to the labor force. About 22 percent of these (13 percent of all those interviewed) say that they cannot work either because of a physical disability (21 percent) or alcohol/drug problem (1.5 percent). A few find child care responsibilities to be a problem (3 percent). The other 20 percent appear to be so weakly attached to the labor force that they do not see working as important or necessary (Table 3.2).

Of the one in four Ohio homeless who report holding a job any time during the month preceding the interview, 25 percent were employed in full-time, permanent jobs (one in 16 of all homeless). The others have worked at odd jobs requiring little long-term commitment to the labor force. One-half of these also report that, in the past, they typically held this kind of job rather than full-time employment.

When asked why they are now unemployed, 19 percent of the Ohio homeless report that they quit their last jobs (Table 3.3). Others indicate that employment that ended involuntarily was temporary (30 percent) or ended due to a plant,

TABLE 3.2. Recent employment history

	%	n
Worked last month? (Yes)	24.7	233
Type of job		
Permanent full-time	25.0	
Permanent part-time	10.3	
Day labor	34.9	
Temporary job	24.1	
Other	5.2	
Is this the work you usually do? (yes)	50.2	117

Source: Ohio Department of Mental Health 1985.

closing or layoff (12 percent) or because they were fired (16 percent). Personal problems ended employment for the remainder: poor health (11 percent), alcohol/drugs (6 percent), poor mental health (4 percent), or incarceration (2 percent).

INCOME

Being homeless and dependent on others for food and shelter may or may not result from a lack of adequate income. The media have made much of the "new poor," defined loosely as those who once held rewarding jobs, but as a result of recession or cutbacks in government programs are now, through no fault of their own, without adequate income. For this group, some of whom become homeless, poverty is a new, and often a temporary, experience. With job placement, retraining, relocation assistance, or through their own job search efforts, most could soon return to the labor force. However, most of the homeless are not in this category. Instead, as we have seen, most are only loosely attached to the labor force. Many have always been poor or nearly poor.

The financial circumstances of the homeless become apparent when their sources of income are compared to those of the much larger class of which they are a part. In 1983, about two-thirds of U.S. householders (heads of families and unrelated individuals), aged 25 to 60, living below the poverty line had some earned income,[2] but of the Ohio homeless, only 17 percent gave earnings as their primary income source and only one-fourth had worked for pay within the month. Two percent of the poor householders reported having no current income; but 37 percent of the homeless said they had no income.

TABLE 3.3. Reasons given for loss of job

Reason last job ended	%
Temporary	29.8
Plant closing, layoff	11.5
Fired	16.3
Quit	19.2
Poor health	11.1
Alcohol/drug problem	5.8
Poor mental health	4.3
Jail/prison	1.9
Other	—
Don't know	—
Total	100.0
(*n*)	(208)

Questions were asked of those who once worked but are not now working.
Source: Ohio Department of Mental Health 1985.

Unlike most poor people who lack earned income, relatively few of the homeless can rely on public welfare, private charity, pensions, or social security. Of the Ohio homeless, one-fourth indicated that public assistance or charity was their primary source of income; and another 14 percent gave social security or pensions as their primary source. Of all U.S. poor aged 25 to 64, on the other hand, more than three-fourths report some income other than earnings, including 36 percent who receive public assistance (Federal Aid to Families with Dependent Children or state general assistance), 12 percent who receive Social Security, six percent who get Supplemental Security Income (SSI), 16 percent who receive income from pensions, alimony, annuities, or similar sources, and 17 percent who receive other transfer payments. Although the different forms in which information or income sources are provided make exact comparisons impossible, it is clear that the homeless are poorer than the poor in general. Despite being 20 times more likely than the average poor adult to have no source of current income, the homeless also are apparently less likely than other poor to be receiving income from sources that ordinarily substitute for earnings.

For those who do receive benefits, payment amounts are not, in most cases, sufficient to pay the rent on a modest dwelling unit. In Ohio, for a four-person household, the fraction of AFDC devoted to shelter (as established by the state) has been estimated at 42 percent of the typical market rent for a modest but physically standard apartment. The comparable ratio for a single elderly person receiving SSI is 70 percent (Newman and Schnare 1985). General relief payments are much smaller; so that, in many cases, the total payment is less than the monthly rent for a modest apartment.

Most of the homeless in Ohio are single males, who would not be eligible for Aid to Families with Dependent Children (AFDC) but could qualify for General Relief (provided they meet state residency requirements and obtain a permanent address) and federal food stamps.[3] Bureaucratic delays or foul-ups may have caused some homeless not to receive assistance to which they were entitled. It remains a mystery, however, why there are so many homeless who have no source of income.

Several things may account for the failure to take advantage of welfare programs. Some of the homeless may not be able to tolerate long lines, waiting, paper work, and probing investigations required to obtain assistance. Others may be unaware of programs for which they are eligible. In Ohio, interviews with human service caseworkers suggest that only rarely does the lack of a fixed address constitute grounds for denying benefits. Indeed, residency requirements typically are interpreted to mean ''intention to remain in the present county'' and not that a person is a legal resident, as would be required in registering to vote. Impressionistic evidence from many service providers suggests that the welfare system is quite flexible in dealing with homeless people.

Other explanations can be suggested for the lack of income from public services. Some homeless may have their eligibility for benefits interrupted due to intermittent paid labor or frequent moves. Others may not understand the welfare system sufficiently to access its resources. They may not know where to seek assistance, may receive incorrect information about how to proceed, or may not be persistent enough to extract from the system that to which they are entitled.

In general, the homeless are people who, today and in the recent past, have too little income to sustain a permanent residence or to meet other basic needs. Even the three of ten homeless people in Ohio with some earnings from work are unable to earn enough to pay for permanent housing.

SOCIAL CONTACT

For some observers, one of the defining characteristics of the homeless person is isolation from friends, relatives, and what they regard as the "mainstream" of society. The image of homeless people as isolated is consistent with the belief that those who have a social network for support can avoid being homeless by turning to family or friends.

Recent research suggests, however, that homeless people have considerably more contact with family or friends than might be expected (cf. Segal, Baumohl, and Johnson 1977). This was confirmed in the Ohio study. Two-fifths (42 percent) of the homeless have had some form of contact with relatives during the last week. Seven in ten have contact with friends. On the other hand, contact may not mean material help. Fewer of the homeless had either relatives (36 percent) or friends (55 percent) on whom they said they could count for help.

When asked why they had not maintained contact with friends and relatives, those who had lost contact gave one of these reasons: their friends and relatives would not help if contacted; they did not live close by; they had lost touch with each other; or the homeless person was ashamed of his or her condition. Unwillingness of others to help was the reason given most often (33 percent), by far, for not maintaining contact.

Thus, some homeless people appear to be cut off from personal relationships that serve others well. When most people are short of cash, they borrow from friends or relatives. When a worker is laid off, neighbors and relatives provide odd jobs for cash to help supplement incomes until new jobs are obtained. People really down on their luck may move back home with relatives. Some of the homeless are people who either never had or have exhausted these normal sources of social support.

Where this informal support system is absent, the reason may lie in the behavior of friends and relatives or of the homeless themselves—a product of prolonged poverty and the heavy claims that this can make on close relationships. Many of the Ohio homeless acknowledge that they eventually wore out their welcome with friends and family. These include those who are chronic alcoholics or drug abusers, have severe mental health problems, or otherwise make themselves unwelcome guests. The expropriation of scarce family resources for alcohol or drugs damages these relationships. Violence against members deteriorates the family fabric. Overcrowded living conditions add to tensions. Although there has been little systematic study of the family relationship of the homeless, anecdotal and impressionistic accounts suggest that families sometimes put up with a lot of abuse before finally expelling a member. Such accounts also suggest that families can be quite forgiving, repeatedly taking the troubled member back.

Of course, homeless people not only abuse their families and friends, but are sometimes abused in return. Women may be beaten by husbands until forced to leave home. A parent may abuse a teenager physically or psychologically. For some, isolation is a relief.

Those homeless who lack a viable social network of friends or relatives must cope with difficult circumstances in virtual isolation. As time goes by, that isolation may grow. This is only partially supported by the Ohio survey, however—the longer homeless, the greater the passage of time since they last contacted relatives; but, the duration of homelessness and the time since the last interaction with friends are unrelated. This pattern could mean simply that homeless people, like others, are not free to choose their relatives but are free to make friends. Relatives may eventually be alienated, whereas new friends may be selected, cultivated, or abandoned at the discretion of individuals.

USE OF HUMAN SERVICES

Because many of the homeless have only weakly developed personal support systems and cannot provide adequately for themselves, if they are to receive assistance, it must come from the formal system of human service agencies. At one time or another, most homeless must rely on shelter providers and soup kitchen operators. Although no research exists to confirm this, the high turnover rates at shelters and long lines at soup kitchens offer impressionistic support. In Ohio, this impression is supported by testimony of the homeless themselves—more than one-half have eaten at a community kitchen (61 percent) or stayed in a shelter (56 percent) during the past month.

The homeless necessarily rely heavily on help that is free and has no income or other eligibility requirements. Interviews conducted with hospital administrators and surveys of the general population in Ohio suggest that many people undergoing severe personal crisis involving mental or physical health, and sometimes non-health-related problems, show up at hospital emergency rooms. Nearly 23 percent of the adult population in the state reported, for example, having been to an emergency room in the past year.[4] It is not surprising that the homeless in Ohio pass through this open door at a higher rate: 25 percent report visiting an emergency room in the last month.

For the homeless, use of the emergency room often is not self-initiated but results from actions by others. Police departments that arrest drunks often take them to emergency rooms for their safety, and, in the case of substance abusers, to reduce liability risk for the city. In communities with no emergency psychiatric care facilities, homeless people who lose emotional control may be taken to regular hospitals for later referral to psychiatric treatment centers. Because many homeless people are exposed to the weather while living on the streets or because shelters at which they are staying require them to leave in daylight hours, they are occasionally taken to emergency rooms for treatment of frostbite, food poisoning, malnutrition, or other medical problems. The emergency room also treats homeless people who are victims of street or domestic violence.

Although homeless people are more likely than others to have a history of institutionalization for mental health reasons, a relatively low proportion have used services provided through community mental health centers (CMHCs) in Ohio during the past twelve months. In fact, the proportion who use these community facilities is much smaller than the proportion who have been institutionalized (see Chapter 5). The rare contact with CMHCs may mean several things. First, CMHCs have no tradition of working with homeless clients. Interviews with human service providers in Ohio showed, for example, that few CMHC administrators had ever dealt with more than a handful of homeless people. Because CMHC caseloads are so heavy relative to their resources, the centers tend to treat clients who will derive the most benefit or show most rapid progress or those who have health insurance that can reimburse centers for treatment (e.g., third-party payments from Medicare). Most of the homeless are not considered by service providers to be in this group. Second, concerning those homeless who have been or are severely ill, there appears to be considerable discontinuity between release from a psychiatric hospital and continuous care provided by a CMHC. As noted by others, a number of the formerly hospitalized fall through the cracks after release (Bachrach 1984a). Third, many homeless people, who might be assumed to need services, do not believe that visiting CMHCs is in their best interest. Instead, these services are viewed as an intrusion on their freedom.

JAIL

Homeless people may be likelier than the average person to wind up in jail, either as a result of deviant behavior associated with their adaptation to such a life or because their struggle for survival brings them into conflict with the law (Lamb 1982a). Some homeless may break the law to acquire basic necessities such as food, shelter, and clothing. Detention might occur either because they were caught in the act of committing a crime or because they provoked arrest to secure better shelter and a meal at the local jailhouse. In some places today as in most places in the past, homeless people may be arrested simply because they are engaging in unproductive activities: loitering or "vagrancy."[5] And finally, alcohol and substance abuse, common among homeless people, may lead to arrest.

Homeless people do appear to be more likely than others to be jailed. Among the general population, about 270 of every 1,000 people at some time have been placed in detention or incarceration (Rabkin 1979); the homeless in Ohio have a rate more than twice as high (590 per 1,000).

Homeless people are most often arrested for minor offenses such as public intoxication and disorderly conduct, but occasionally for more serious misdemeanors and felonies involving violence or crimes against property. Are homeless people a serious threat to the well-being of the community? In fact, based on statistics for one city in Ohio (Youngstown), with few exceptions, the homeless not only appear to constitute little threat to the community, but are perhaps less dangerous than the average person. Between 60 and 80 percent of the homeless arrested in that city between 1977 and 1984 were charged with either public intoxication or drug abuse. Of those charged with substance abuse, only one homeless person annually was charged with a drug-related offense. Anywhere from three to fourteen homeless people annually were charged with disorderly conduct and resisting arrest. These offenses almost always are associated with alcohol or drugs. If charges for disorderly conduct and resisting arrest are combined with substance abuse, then at least three-fourths of the arrests of homeless people were either drug- or alcohol-related.

"Loitering and suspicion," when charged against a homeless person, typically means that the police are arresting someone because he or she needs food and shelter or is bothering residents, merchants, or consumers in a business district. Only a handful of homeless people were charged with these minor offenses. This suggests that arrest is not a tactic commonly used by homeless people in this area to obtain food and shelter.

The remaining arrests of the homeless (accounting for about one-fifth of those arrested) were for serious crimes either against property or persons. Within this category, property crimes greatly outnumber crimes of violence. Property crimes involved mostly theft and receiving stolen property. Violent crimes not on the FBI's serious crime index usually involve assault. The most serious crimes, those eleven reported by the FBI as serious felonies, rarely involve the homeless, except as victims. Grand theft, robbery, felonious assault, and murder were among the few such charges made against homeless persons.

Most of the homeless people who ended up in jail were victims of their own "crimes"—that is, alcohol abuse. Only a small minority are dangerous to others, being involved in violent crimes against others or in property crimes that might precipitate violence.

MOBILITY

Homeless people seem to be constantly on the move, either from town to town or from place to place within a community. Some move because this is their chosen life style. Others move to improve their circumstances, if only in a small way. Better public welfare benefits may attract homeless people from states that do not have as much to offer. Word that jobs are available in other communities may encourage homeless migration. Relatives, not seen for many years, may offer to take in a homeless person with promises of forgiveness. Still others may move to avoid difficulties. Local police may seek the arrest of a homeless person for suspicion of committing a crime. Northern winters may drive the homeless south to warmer climates. A favorite condemned tenement once offering shelter may be razed, displacing the homeless in the process. Homeless people themselves, competing for scarce resources—a favorite shelter, a source of fresh food, a place of warmth on a subway grate—may force others to move along.

No studies have been made, to our knowledge, of patterns of movement by homeless people. However, the Ohio survey does offer some limited insight on their mobility.

The homeless in Ohio (see Table 3.4) are, as expected, more mobile than the general population. Two-fifths indicated that they were permanent residents of the county or city where they were encountered, while another 24 percent reported living in that jurisdiction for at least a year. By way of comparison, only 15 percent of Ohio households interviewed for the 1980 U.S. census said they had changed their county of residence within the last five years (U.S. Bureau of the Census 1980).

Those not originally from the county or city in which they were interviewed came from a wide variety of places. Over one-third migrated from another Ohio county. However, over one-fourth migrated from one of the states contiguous with Ohio (i.e., Pennsylvania, West Virginia, Kentucky, Indiana, and Michigan), and the remainder (38 percent) came from other states.

If the place of interview and previous place of residence are mapped, two distinct patterns of movement are found within the state. One pattern is for rural homeless people to find their way to the larger metropolitan areas. Another is from one large metropolitan area to another.

With little to tie them down, or fleeing some personal crisis, a substantial portion of the homeless population is on the move.

CONCLUSION

Among the most striking findings of the Ohio survey is the lack of current income among the homeless, even when compared to other poor people. Not only are the homeless far less likely than the poor in general to be working; but fewer

TABLE 3.4. Mobility in the homeless population

	%	n
Number of places stayed during past month		
1–2	57.1	559
3–4	25.0	245
5–6	7.0	69
7–8	2.0	20
9+	5.8	57
No answer	3.0	29
Total	99.9	979

Mean number of places—3.3
Median number of places—2

Length of time Living in County:		
Less than 1 week	10.0	98
1–4 weeks	12.9	126
1–6 months	8.3	81
7–12 months	4.6	45
12 months+	23.9	234
Permanent resident	39.6	388
No answer	0.7	7
Total	100.0	979

Source: Ohio Department of Mental Health 1985.

are looking for work. When unemployed, they are also less likely than others to be receiving some form of public assistance or other income support. In many cases also lacking support from family or friends, most will not be able to live on their own without first finding new sources of income.

Despite their poverty, the homeless find various ways of meeting their most basic needs—for food and shelter. Congregating in specific inner-city neighborhoods, with their patchwork systems of shelters and other services, helps the homeless meet survival needs. However, the homeless habitat can also be dangerous. The longer people must subsist in such surroundings, the less likely they will return to more normal patterns of living.

Finally, this glimpse of how the homeless live poses questions that we cannot answer. Much of what we would like to know—about the movement into and out of homelessness; about the interactions between homeless people and official institutions, including police, the shelters, and other human services agencies that might help them; about their past and present relationships with family and friends; and how and why the homeless move from place to place—can be learned only through longitudinal tracking of this population.

NOTES

1. This quotation was taken from a letter written by an unemployed man to President Roosevelt in 1935. See McElvaine 1983, p. 2.

2. The comparison is with this group of households because their age range most closely matches that of the homeless; they constitute nearly 80 percent of all poor households (U.S. Census Bureau, *Current Population Reports*, P-60, 1983, Table 34). The Ohio homeless were asked only to name their *primary* source of income, but households surveyed by the Bureau of the Census were asked to name all sources. Therefore, the comparison of income sources cannot be exact.

3. In Ohio, single adults, 18 and over, without children, may receive approximately $120 per month if they demonstrate financial need and are prepared to register with the state employment service as being available for work. In some states, younger able-bodied adults are not eligible for general assistance. For example, in Massachusetts, individuals between the ages of 18 and 44 may receive general assistance only if they are disabled or handicapped and, if 45 or older, only if they are "unemployable and destitute."

4. This percentage was derived from county-level needs assessment data provided by the Division of Program Evaluation and Research, Ohio Department of Mental Health.

5. Although loitering and vagrancy are no longer considered crimes, police departments sometimes arrest people for these behaviors, using other criminal charges, such as simple assault when resisting an officer's suggestion to move along.

4

HOW DID THEY
GET THAT WAY?

There are many ways to become homeless. This chapter looks at the process by which people wind up with no place to live. It is about causes, but mainly proximate rather than ultimate causes, and its focus is on the homeless individual, rather than on the larger social structures and norms that sustain, tolerate, and justify homelessness and other kinds of severe deprivation. It is useful to know to what extent there are typical chains of events or causal sequences leading to homelessness in order to fashion effective prevention strategies.

Describing these sequences deepens our understanding of who the homeless are and what they want and need and confronts some of the more troubling questions about the homeless: Is homelessness a sudden break with normal life or the culmination of a gradual descent? Or to ask a slightly different question: Are the homeless, for the most part, "normal" people after a run of bad luck or a predisposed, vulnerable group? These are questions about the degree to which people control their lives or whether homelessness is the kind of "disease" that might strike anyone, including ourselves.

These questions are addressed with data from the Ohio survey, compared where possible with findings of other studies. A set of personal case histories, developed through in-depth discussions with homeless people and those who have aided them, help illustrate the main findings.

WHY PEOPLE SAY THEY ARE HOMELESS

Although the reasons people give for being homeless do not reveal all the causes, they provide a useful starting point. When the Ohio homeless were asked to give the major reason why they "no longer have a permanent or regular home," nearly one-half named what could be classified as economic or financial factors (rent problems, eviction, unemployment, loss of government benefits), one-fourth cited personal crises (disasters, deinstitutionalization, family conflict or dissolution) that may or may not have had an economic component, and a much smaller proportion (7 percent) named alcohol or drug problems. About 6 percent gave answers such as, "I just like to move around," suggesting that this was a preferred or chosen condition. One in eight offered no clear answer (Table 4.1).

Although the stated reasons for homelessness seem to offer a convenient basis for classification, the groups are less distinct than expected (Table 4.2).

• For example, 40 percent of those offering economic explanations were without current income when interviewed; but so too were 30 percent of those citing personal crises, 35 percent of those naming alcohol or drugs, and 38 percent of those who said they liked to wander. Exactly the same proportion of each group (17–18 percent) reported employment earnings as their primary current income source.

• Those citing personal crises as causes are younger, on average, than other groups, and those citing alcohol or drugs average a bit older than the others; but in all four groups, there is a wide range of ages.

TABLE 4.1. Reasons given by Ohio homeless for having no permanent home

Reason	Percentage Responding
Economic, financial	48.1
Unemployment	21.8
Problems paying rent	13.9
Eviction	9.6
Government benefits stopped	2.8
Personal crises	26.3
Family conflict	13.3
Family dissolution	8.0
Deinstitutionalization	2.5
Disaster	2.5
Alcohol, drug problems	7.3
Preferred life	6.1
None; not clear	12.2
Total Sample	100.0

Source: Ohio Department of Mental Health 1985.

TABLE 4.2. Characteristics of Ohio homeless by major reason given for homelessness

	Stated reason for homelessness				
	Economic, financial	Personal crisis	Alcohol, drugs	Preference	All
Age					
18–29	32	44	21	32	35
30–39	31	25	21	20	28
40–49	16	14	25	27	17
50–59	16	11	24	7	13
60+	5	5	8	13	6
Education					
0–8 Years	20	12	20	22	17
9–11 Years	35	43	39	30	37
High school graduate	33	29	21	33	30
Some college	11	12	15	13	12
College graduate	1	3	4	2	2
Marital status					
Married/living together	14	9	4	8	11
Separated/divorced	39	40	65	35	39
Widowed	5	5	3	3	4
Never married	42	46	28	53	45
Current income					
None	40	30	35	38	37
Welfare; charity	27	41	20	12	25
Family; friends	2	2	1	3	2

TABLE 4.2. (Continued)

	Stated reason for homelessness				
	Economic, financial	Personal crisis	Alcohol, drugs	Preference	All
Social security; pension	9	13	17	25	14
Earnings	17	18	18	17	17
Refused; other	5	7	8	4	6
Days homeless					
1–7	42	49	39	52	44
8–30	10	11	4	10	10
31–180	34	27	27	40	28
>180	14	13	28	20	15
Ever employed					
Worked in last month	27	27	27	40	28
Yes; not in last month	65	60	65	55	63
No; never	8	13	8	5	10

Ever hospitalized for mental health					
Yes	21	35	42	32	30
No	78	65	55	65	69
No answer	1	1	3	3	1
Sought help for drinking					
Yes	23	25	68	20	27
No	75	72	28	80	71
No answer	2	3	4	0	3
Trouble with drugs					
Yes	4	5	8	0	5
No	23	30	21	17	26
No medication in last month	73	65	70	83	70
Relatives you can count on					
Yes	34	38	35	25	36
No, can't count on	42	51	44	32	43
No, none	23	11	20	40	20
No answer	1	0	1	3	1

Source: Ohio Department of Mental Health 1985.

• There is very little difference among the four groups in education. Once again, the more telling point is probably that each group is diverse, including a significant minority of college graduates along with a majority who did not complete high school.

Looking for any characteristic that would sharply distinguish members of one group from the others is, for the most part, fruitless. Those who give unemployment or other economic or financial factors as the primary reason for their condition are less likely than members of the other three classes to have been hospitalized for mental health problems (although 21 percent of them do report being hospitalized); but on no other obvious dimension of demography or personal history are they at all distinctive. Those citing personal crises are, as noted, a bit younger on average and are more likely than those in the other three groups to cite welfare payments as their primary income source; but again, there is no personal characteristic or set of characteristics that would flag them as a distinct group.

The few homeless giving alcohol or drug problems or a preference for mobility as the main reason for their condition are closer to being distinctive groups, but are far from homogeneous groups. Those with alcohol or drug problems are more likely than others to have been homeless for two years or longer. Nearly two-thirds are separated or divorced, compared to 40 percent or fewer in the other groups. One-third are over 50 years of age, versus less than 20 percent of those in other groups. Also, apart from those naming deinstitutionalization as the reason for their homelessness, they are more likely than any other group to report being hospitalized for mental health reasons. Those suggesting that homelessness is part of a preferred living pattern are more likely than others to have worked in the last month and less likely to have been married or to have relatives they can count on; in fact, 40 percent claim they have no relatives. Having noted these differences, however, even those two groups must still be characterized as demographically heterogeneous and not easily differentiable from other groups of homeless.

Multiple and sequential causation

The different reasons offered for homelessness do not define sociologically distinctive groups. This begins to suggest a complex pattern of causation. There may not be many people for whom homelessness is clearly the result of a single event or personal attribute. Job loss may lead to family conflict—and a battered wife flees her husband. Alcoholism or severe mental illness may contribute to a firing and, subsequently, eviction for failure to pay rent. Chronic economic deprivation puts a young person at risk for drug problems. The preference for a life of constant movement develops as an adaptation to the lack of support from family and friends. The extent to which the diverse causes of homelessness may be combined and intertwined is illustrated by recent events in the life of one homeless woman (in the box below).[1]

WILLA MAE

Willa Mae and her three children are separated from one another now—staying with several different friends while she looks for an apartment. This 30-year-old black woman and her family have suffered through a series of crises, spread over several years.

She first came to Ohio to live with her brother after graduating from high school in Georgia thirteen years ago. She was married six months later to a man who attacked her when he was drunk and, four years ago, slit her throat. Willa Mae often wears scarves and turtlenecks to cover up the scars.

After eight years of marriage, she fled, taking the children to Georgia to live with her parents. Shortly after her divorce, Willa Mae's brother asked her to return to Ohio, to help care for his wife who was dying of cancer. After the woman's death, Willa Mae stayed with her brother, then moved into her own apartment.

Willa Mae does not have a job. Her only source of income is a welfare check which, she says, is not enough to cover her family's basic needs.

Their most recent misfortune left the family out in the street. They were evicted, illegally, from their apartment in June 1984. At the time Willa Mae was one month behind in her rent. However, the landlord failed to give her the required three days' notice in writing or to file a formal complaint with the court. Instead, he moved her belongings to an open garage while she was visiting her daughter at a Pittsburgh hospital. "He pitched out a lot of my furniture, causing damage to a television set and breaking tables and lamps," she said. Legal services' attorneys tried to recover her possessions but discovered that anything of value had been either broken or stolen from the open garage. Among the stolen items were $250 worth of clothes that her former mother-in-law had purchased for the children a week before they were evicted.

Willa Mae believes her landlord threw her out because she refused to re-sign her Section 8 rent subsidy contract for another year. (Section 8 is a federally funded subsidized housing program that pays the difference between 30 percent of a tenant's adjusted income and the total rent.) In her case, the total monthly rent was $327 (not including utilities), of which she paid $60. She did not want to re-sign her contract because she believed her utility bills were too high and intended to move.

The money Willa Mae would have used to pay her rent or move went instead for transportation costs to a Pittsburgh hospital. A few weeks before the family was evicted, her daughter fell down the apartment steps, shattering her elbow. Several operations were necessary to put the elbow back together.

When Willa Mae talked to Section 8 officials, she was told she would have "to find a place on her own." She said, "without a car, money, or clothes, they did not give me very many options." She applied to the public housing authority for an apartment but was told she did not qualify as an emergency case. She then followed up leads from her friends concerning apartments they saw advertised for rent. In each case, the landlord would tell her to call back; but when she did so, she was told the apartment had already been rented.

Eventually, she found an apartment she considered satisfactory; but Section 8 officials could not approve the rent payments, since it had only two bedrooms. They have insisted that, because of her family's size, she find a three-bedroom apartment. Meanwhile, she does not have a place to stay.

Last year, her son was hit by a car. His legs and arms are still badly scarred. His head has permanent bald spots where it scraped the pavement, and he suffers frequent memory losses. His mother says that he wakes up screaming in the night from painful headaches.

Willa Mae's oldest daughter "is angry at everyone. She has temper tantrums and is rebelling against everything. She tries to strike back by cursing and fighting. When she starts to scream in school, the teachers can't seem to stop her," according to Willa Mae.

As soon as she finds another apartment, Willa Mae plans to enroll in a two-year food management program, resuming an education interrupted by her son's accident.

Such a multiplicity of causal factors invites disagreement. In the absence of data that would be provided by large-scale systematic surveys of the homeless population, political ideology and advocacy have played a large role in shaping opinion. So conflicting and complex is the evidence on causality that some would conclude the homeless have little in common but their homelessness—a symptom or syndrome without a common or consistent etiology. To accept such a conclusion would probably mean abandoning the search for a strategy of prevention. It would also leave a clean slate on which those less constrained by evidence would continue to write their own oversimplified interpretations and prescriptions. We have some obligation, therefore, to sort out the evidence on causality, casting doubt on the more one-sided views of homelessness, while searching for often-repeated sequences and useful generalizations.

INSTITUTIONS OR INDIVIDUALS?

Explanations for homelessness divide into two categories: those emphasizing the effects of social institutions and public policies and those emphasizing attributes of the individuals who are homeless. Those who stress external factors include those who might be expected to have ideologically distinctive positions on other issues; the same is true of those who stress internal factors.

Institutions and policies

One view emphasizing external institutional factors is offered by Leo Srole, in his introduction to a study of New York City's homeless prepared by a liberal advocacy group, the Community Service Society of New York. Srole characterizes the homeless as "the 'fall out' rejects of a highly competitive, cornucopian socioeconomic system that cannot mobilize the fiscal wherewithal and organizational talents for quasi-family care of its casualties" (Baxter and Hopper 1981, ii). Srole's failure to specify more precisely the process by which people become systemic casualties, or why some people are vulnerable, makes this difficult to verify or reject as stated.

A more recent report on homelessness in New York State, prepared by the state's Department of Social Services, offers a second, and fairly specific, version of what may be called the "institutional" hypothesis. Based on a survey of shelter operators, this report concludes that: "the sudden dramatic increase in this state in the numbers of homeless people whose only handicap is poverty cannot simply be explained with reference to social pathology or personal mismanagement. Last year,... more than 85 percent of those in emergency shelters had no known mental health problems, 63 percent required no supported or enriched living arrangements, 80 percent suffered from no chemical dependency, and at least as many had never been institutionalized" (N.Y. Dept. of Social Services 1984, 32).

The New York State report blames homelessness there primarily on a sharp drop in the low-income housing supply (especially in New York City), a sharp rise in poverty and unemployment, and the combination of high housing costs with inadequate public assistance shelter allowances. This version of the institutional/external hypothesis is more readily subject than Srole's to empirical verification or rejection.

Anna Kondratas, a research fellow at the conservative Heritage Foundation, discounts one set of institutional factors as causes of homelessness but blames another. In her view, "the root causes of increasing homelessness are not unemployment and federal budget cuts.... Rather, the causes are ill-conceived mental health and housing policies—on the federal, state, and local levels" (Kondratas 1985, 13). Her reading of the evidence suggests that deinstitutionalization of the mentally ill and the loss of low-income housing stock due to urban development, gentrification, and rent control "are the chief causes of homelessness in the early 1980's."

Internal factors and individual responsibility

It is not surprising that a more traditional view of the reasons for homelessness survives and is supported by some analyses. This view attributes some or most homelessness either to individual weakness or to individual choice—in any case, to factors internal to the homeless themselves.

One version of the internal factors hypothesis (that many, perhaps most, homeless are either mentally ill or addicted to drugs or alcohol) complements and is consistent with Kondratas's argument that many homeless would be institutionalized under the hospital admissions practices prevailing before 1963. In fact, she concludes that, "the vast majority of today's homeless ... are ... either dependent on drugs or alcohol, or they are mentally ill . . ." (1985a, 1). In essence, homelessness results when society fails to provide continuous custodial care for a certain proportion of the population who, due to constitutional weaknesses, cannot fend for themselves or rely on family or friends for shelter. This view directly contradicts that offered in the 1983 New York State report.

Another explanation for homelessness emphasizing individual rather than institutional failings focuses on domestic turmoil and violence and other problems stemming from personal relationships. Many homeless people, in this view, are running away from unpleasant or unbearable personal circumstances. Their homelessness is recent and is likely to be transitory.

On closer inspection, this version of the internal factors hypothesis, like the first version, is linked to changes in institutions and social norms. The extent to which homelessness results from personal relationships depends not only on the incidence of domestic conflict but also, and perhaps more directly, on prevailing social norms governing reactions to such conflict and on the availability of various forms of support to those involved, including emergency shelter. HUD (U.S. Dept of HUD 1984) found that shelters for battered women and their children (a relatively recent social innovation) accounted for about 7 percent of all emergency shelter beds nationwide. Another 10 percent were reserved for runaway youth. Some of those sheltered in such facilities would, in past years, have turned instead to relatives or friends; and others would have remained in troubled family situations. Neither would have been counted as homeless.

A third, less benign, version of the "internal factors" hypothesis views some homelessness as a manifestation of social deviance and, to that degree at least, a voluntary condition. This view holds that many homeless people are an inevitable flotsam of social misfits, criminals, and those whose urge to wander is stronger than their need to secure permanent shelter, an explanation consistent with the traditional image of the hobo but less in fashion today because it cannot easily be reconciled with the apparent rise in numbers of homeless. However, some researchers have attributed at least part of the increase in homelessness to the collapse of the 1960s "counterculture," which for a time tolerated and supported such people (cf. Harris and Bergman 1983).

The most sophisticated and yet extreme version of the "individual factors" hypothesis may be that put forward by Thomas Main (1983a). Using studies of New York City shelter populations as the basis, Main argues that homelessness in that city is "at least three very different problems:[11] former mental patients and other mentally ill; alcohol and drug abusers; and "economic only" cases who suffer from no disability but find the shelters "attractive" relative to whatever alternative habitats are available to them. Many in the third category are "higher-functioning young men," who are "not chronically homeless, and are not undomiciled at the time of coming to the shelters" (p. 21). Main's classification ignores the large numbers of families and women among New York City's homeless. Nor does he directly address the possible roles of housing costs, welfare policies, or institutional factors other than deinstitutionalization in creating homelessness. Indeed, Main argues that because the ideology of advocacy groups interprets homelessness as a matter "of systemic failure, rather than individual responsibility," they cannot come to grips with the "special case of 'economic only' clients" (p. 23). Although Main would not turn away members of this group seeking shelter, he believes "another, more humane way must be found for 'deterring' higher functioning clients from using the shelters as anything but a last resort" (p. 27). He proposes a work requirement. For Main, "the fact of the matter is that the homeless, like the poor, we will always have with us. The only question is how to help them without encouraging them in their pathologies and dependency" (p. 28).

We are thus faced with the problem of adding up, sorting out, or trying to reconcile, a number of partial and, in some cases, conflicting explanations. Having observed that the causes of homelessness are typically multiple and sequential, we might be tempted to merely acknowledge that each view holds true for some portion of the homeless. However, to decide what public policies are most appropriate to deal with homelessness, it would be very helpful to know at least which causal sequences are most common and what accounts for the apparent surge of homelessness in this decade. Thus, we ask: What evidence is there from systematic discussions with a representative group of the homeless themselves in support of one or another hypothesis?

SORTING OUT CAUSES

The Ohio survey results strongly suggest that the extreme poverty of this group has played a major role in their becoming homeless. As noted in the preceding chapter, the homeless are many times more likely than other poor people to have no source of current income; and yet, they are also less likely than other poor to be receiving public welfare, Social Security, or SSI payments that ordinarily substitute for earned income. Whether their lack of income, or material support from relatives or friends is recent or of long standing, it contributes directly to their present condition. And, where other causes are present, the lack of income compounds their effects.

Unemployment and poverty

Whether the homeless are fleeing from some personal disaster or not, whether mentally ill or addicted or not (whatever the other events or attributes contributing to their homelessness), they are poor. They are poor and often isolated from the usual sources of help: family, friends, private charity, and public welfare. Poverty both compounds their other problems and contributes directly to their lack of reliable shelter.

Of the testable "institutional" hypotheses, the New York State report's attribution of rising homelessness to rising unemployment and poverty, combined with inadequate public assistance, appears to be more consistent than others with results of the Ohio survey. The fact of very high unemployment in that region after 1980, combined with the direct testimony of the homeless themselves, suggests that economic dislocation, and the failure to provide adequate public financial relief, have put many people out of their homes.[2] Some of these are unemployed for the first time in their adult lives; having exhausted whatever unemployment benefits and personal savings they had, unable for a variety of reasons to find new work, perhaps unwilling to accept welfare or charity from friends and relatives, they have moved by stages from a secure, stable existence to the margin of extreme deprivation. Recent work on the long-term impacts of massive job losses on individuals and families suggests that, after several years, a substantial minority of laid-off workers in this region are without work and have suffered severe economic losses (Buss and Redburn 1985). Some laid-off workers are homeless for relatively short periods as they move about in search of work. Others become chronically vulnerable to spells of joblessness and homelessness, as they become less and less attached to the labor force (see case study in box below and the discussion of "work and income" in Chapter 3). And, some who are homeless primarily for economic reasons may never have had a seemingly secure career job, may always have been part of the marginal labor force, and therefore were always vulnerable to spells of unemployment.

EDMUND

Edmund was evicted from his last residence because he couldn't pay his rent or utility bills with the $106 he received monthly from the Welfare Department. After hitching a ride from his home to the Rescue Mission, four miles away, he went to the nearest Soldiers and Sailors Relief Office.

As a World War II veteran, he hoped to get help, but, he said, a young woman working there told him to "get a job." Then he smiled, "but she ain't working there no more. She was fired after I found the head man."

This 60-year-old white man believes that no one will hire him for permanent work because he is too old. "After you pass twenty-five, employers don't want you anymore." For the last ten years, he has survived by working odd jobs, "bumming" food, and sleeping wherever he could find shelter. In the last five months, people that know him in the town where he was born and raised have given him food and "one guy put a bed in a truck garage for me to sleep on."

He stood up and pulled out his wallet, which contained a piece of paper. "Let me show you what I get for fighting for my country. Let me show you what it is to be an American." The paper was a 1984 notice from the county's welfare office stating that he was no longer eligible to receive cash or food stamps from general relief because he did not have a place to stay.

Edmund plans to move to a Soldiers and Sailors Relief Home when the Veteran's Administration confirms his eligibility.

In 1982 he entered the Salvation Army's Drug and Rehabilitation Center. "I don't have a drinking problem, I just told them that to get out of the weather," he explained. He spent only one month there because, he said, he couldn't take the rules and regulations.

In the past, Edmund was a truck driver. For 33 years he worked for one company. They "went broke" in 1972. "The crooks owed me $2,500 for the loads I hauled. I had to go to the National Labor Relations Board and they got me my money." He then worked for another trucking firm, but two years later that firm also went out business.

He has no family life today. He was divorced in 1950. "I beat her up because she was dancing on my money." During the five-year marriage, he says, his wife could pick up his paycheck from the company while he was on the road. She would spend it rather than pay the bills. One day he returned home from work to find that all the utilities had been turned off. "I banged her head in," he claimed.

He then raised his former wife's two sons, who he had adopted during their marriage. She kept custody of her two girls. He hasn't seen his sons in ten years. "I've wrote a few letters to them, that's about it. I'll see them again when I get around to it. I don't bother them 'til I need something."

Edmund does not know what will happen to him in the future. Right now, he'd like "to shoot the U.S. Government, Congress, and the Senate. They're a bunch of crooks. In 1930, you didn't have this kind of trouble. They give our money to the whole world, spend billions on weapons and here we are, starving," he exclaimed. Seven other men sitting in the room with Edmund at the Rescue echoed in agreement.

Work histories help distinguish between those homeless who are newly poor and those who are chronically so. In Ohio, only 9 percent of those who give economic reasons for their lack of secure shelter say they have never worked. Of those who are not working now but once had jobs, about one-fourth lost their last jobs either through layoffs or because the job itself was temporary; the majority lost their jobs for reasons that are more personal (they were fired, quit, or had problems with health, mental health, drinking, or drugs). The relative proportions of these two groups suggest the extent to which the recent wave of industrial layoffs and plant closings account for the current number of homeless in Ohio; it appears that most of those homeless for economic reasons were not laid off after a long period of stable employment but have been marginal to the labor force for an extended period of time.

Circumstantial evidence for the link between poverty and homelessness also can be found in the coincidence between the rise of homelessness in the early 1980s and a sharp rise in the U.S. poverty rate during the same period. The proportion of the population living below the Census Bureau's poverty line rose from about 11.5 percent in 1978 to a high of more than 15 percent in 1983. Palmer and Sawhill (1984) have estimated that recession and budget cuts contributed about equally to the increase. During the Reagan administration, tighter income eligibility limits and sharper benefit offsets for earnings and other income eliminated "an estimated 400,000 to 500,000 AFDC families and nearly a million potential food stamp beneficiaries" and greatly reduced benefits to others (Palmer and Sawhill 1984, 13). Between 1979 and 1982, the proportion of all poor children enrolled in AFDC dropped from 72 to 52 percent (Taylor 1986).

The composition of the poverty population also has shifted, over a somewhat longer period, so that it now includes many more children and families and far fewer elderly than a decade ago. "Since 1970, Social Security benefits have increased by 46 percent in real terms, while wages and salaries—the chief source of income for non-elderly adults and their dependent children—have declined by 7 percent after adjusting for inflation" (Taylor 1986). This shift might help to explain the increasing numbers of families among the homeless as well as the more general rise in numbers. It appears that the lower rungs of the economic ladder became ever more crowded in the late 1970s and early 1980s. As the near-poor became poor, the already-poor became poorer. There was simply no room at the bottom of the ladder for more people scrambling for a fixed or declining number of jobs. It would not be at all surprising if many of the least able or most unlucky were knocked off the ladder and into the street.

Housing and urban redevelopment policies

Housing and urban redevelopment policies have been named as other possible institutional contributors to the apparent increase in homelessness in the 1980s. Circumstantial evidence from the Ohio survey and other studies points to housing problems, stemming largely from lack of income, as a contributing cause; but it is not so easy to trace the housing difficulties of the homeless to specific public housing or redevelopment programs or policies (see the box following). If even the cheapest rents are beyond the means of some individuals and families, this is not necessarily attributable to urban renewal efforts that have reduced the supply of lower-income housing. In Ohio, as in most of the country, most publicly sponsored slum clearance ended nearly two decades ago. Subsequent government efforts to stabilize modest-income neighborhoods by subsidizing private rehabilitation and improving infrastructure may have, in some places, offset or even temporarily reversed the normal process by which older housing filters down from middle-income to lower-income occupancy; but such efforts also may have slowed the rate at which lower-income housing was lost through deterioration and abandonment. Moreover, the number of federally subsidized low-income apartments was increased by one million between 1980 and 1986. Nor, in most parts of the country including Ohio, are local government rent controls a factor affecting the supply of low-income housing. In fact, given the relatively high rental vacancy rates and low rent levels prevalent in Ohio, the housing problems of its poor, and of those who become homeless especially, do not appear to result from an inadequate supply of low-cost housing but, more directly, from lack of income.

MICHAEL

Michael, 22, was laid off from his job two months before arriving at the Rescue Mission, where he had been for several nights. He had worked for five months as a part-time janitor before his layoff, and is not eligible to receive unemployment compensation. At the time of Michael's layoff, his 17-year-old wife was seven months pregnant with their first child.

Out of work and unable to pay the rent on his $250-a-month apartment, Michael was told to be out by December 23. He received assurances from the Urban League that they would pay December's rent; however, the landlord refused to accept this money, because "he just wanted us out." Since the baby was to be born within the month, Michael refused to leave until given a court order. His wife had the baby on schedule, and they were homeless nine days later.

Michael applied for welfare; but he was ruled ineligible for benefits because he would not have a place of residence. The Urban League referred him to an emergency shelter, but they had no vacancies for families. He then went back to the Welfare Department and explained his dilemma. They offered him $263 for the first month's rent when he found an apartment. However, it would take 30 to 45 days after moving into an apartment before the landlord would receive any money; and none of the landlords Michael talked to were willing to cooperate on those terms.

Michael's mother let him stay with her for a few days, and Jan's brother allowed her and the baby to stay with him. They were not separated by family prejudice—Michael is black and Jan is white—but by economics. Michael's mother was also housing his aunt, sister, niece, and nephew and could not afford to keep him. So, after a few days, she asked him to find another place. Because Jan's brother was keeping their grandmother and helping her buy medicine, and had recently lost his job, he could not also afford to keep Jan and the baby. She, too, had to leave within a few days.

Finally, when Michael called the Rescue Mission, in the next county, they did have a vacancy. He has also applied for welfare there and has identified some low-income apartments that require only a security deposit for the first month. It is likely the family will soon have a home.

Meanwhile, Michael is still looking for work in maintenance. If he remains unemployed, he says he will go back to school. Prior to getting his part-time job, he had been enrolled in a medical assistant training course. "I should have stayed in school, but I dropped out when I had a chance to go to work." Jan, who dropped out of school in the ninth grade, plans to pursue her high school diploma and job training when the baby is older.

The couple will celebrate their two-year anniversary this coming March.

If one were to base conclusions on the Ohio situation only, public policies that govern eligibility for housing assistance, and others that directly or indirectly affect the distribution of incomes (but not housing and urban redevelopment policies) would be implicated in homelessness. And, we have noted (in Chapter 2), the rate of homelessness does not seem to vary across the country in a pattern that is associated with variations in the cost or availability of rental housing.

The situation in some areas of the country is different, however. In New York City and in some California cities, rent controls have been blamed for decreased investment in or abandonment of multifamily housing (cf. Downs 1983). In urban areas where government action has contributed to rapid gentrification or to commercial revitalization that displaces older low-cost housing and transient lodging, these policies may have contributed to homelessness. However, recent massive shifts in use and occupancy, such as the rapid reduction in single-room occupancy hotels cited in the New York State (New York Department of Social Services 1984) and other studies, are in the main a response to broad changes in investment incentives, including federal tax policies, not the result of urban renewal or housing programs.[3] In any case, the connection between government urban policies and homelessness is, at best, indirect.

Personal attributes, interpersonal conflicts

Although poverty stands out as a major contributor to homelessness, the Ohio survey confirms that personal attributes or interpersonal conflicts also are involved in many instances of homelessness. A group whose lack of reliable shelter results partly from personal problems, as opposed to the workings of economic and political institutions, are those fleeing from domestic turmoil and violence. Based on testimony by the homeless themselves, family conflict or dissolution is at least a precipitating cause of homelessness for about one in five Ohio homeless (see the box following). HUD's review of local studies suggests that 40 to 50 percent of all instances of homelessness, on an annual basis, can be linked to these or similar types of acute personal crisis. However, because this group tends to be homeless for shorter periods, the proportion of those homeless for such reasons at any single point in time will be smaller (U.S. Dept. of HUD 1984, 26).

HELEN

Helen is about five foot one. Her hair is usually disheveled and she wears baggy clothes. The black rings under her eyes make her look tired. She has taken refuge at the Rescue Mission in part because it is the only place in the area other than the Battered Woman's Shelter that has accommodations for homeless women.

Helen is not a battered wife anymore. After 30 years of marriage to an alcoholic, she left. Having promised her husband early in the marriage that she would stay with him until the children were grown, she walked out when the youngest of their seven children went into the service. Although this was ten years ago, the couple were not legally divorced until last year.

Throughout her marriage, Helen's husband was a heavy drinker. On the many nights when he did not come home, Helen would call hospitals and police stations looking for him. She usually learned that he had been picked up by the police for drinking while driving. In the morning, she would go to the jail and bail him out.

It was the "little things that he used to do that I couldn't take anymore." She said that he once tried to run over her and their daughter with his car. Another time, he threatened her and the children with a large knife. When they locked themselves in a room, he jabbed the knife into the door.

She says that her husband was very unkind to this girl because she was not his own. Helen conceived her first child by a man she was engaged to during World War II. He died in the war. As a result, Helen has remained close to this child. She does not visit her other children because, she says, they live so far away.

After leaving her husband, Helen and her granddaughter went to California, where Helen worked as a live-in maid. When she received word that her eldest daughter's husband had died in Ohio, she and her granddaughter came home for the funeral. Afterward, Helen remained in Ohio.

Helen does not know where she will go when she turns 62 this coming June. At that time she will be eligible for Social Security.

The evidence, however, does not support the view that homelessness results primarily from flaws in the individual or from conflicts between individuals. Explanations that rely on personal attributes or behavior suffer from two principal flaws. First, on closer examination, they generally have an institutional or public policy component. Economic and housing problems contribute to the incidence of personal crises and, even more, to the probability that such crises will precipitate homelessness. Second, because patterns of human behavior change rather slowly, such changes could not possibly account for a rapid rise in the rate of homelessness in a whole society, such as the United States and other industrial countries have recently experienced.

Volunteers

Those who claim to be homeless because they like to move around or who give similar reasons suggesting that theirs is a voluntary condition may come closest to fitting the traditional image (see the box below). However, fewer than one in fifteen homeless people in Ohio gave such answers; and even these responses must be viewed skeptically.

LARRY

For the past fourteen years, Larry has wandered around the country living in flophouses and working at odd jobs. He is amiable and polite. When visited at the Rescue Mission, he was sober. He chose the transient life, he says, because he liked wandering around the country with no responsibilities or commitments to anyone. But, as he reflects on his past, it becomes obvious that his transience is tied to alcohol. In the same breath that he says, "I chose this life and I like it," he interjects in a softer voice, "but my dream wish is to stop drinking and settle down in one place."

Unlike other alcoholics who pass through the Rescue Mission, Larry does not show the kinds of scars often inflicted by alcoholism. At 41, he is still good-looking and maintains a dignity and pride that most of the others at the Mission appear to have lost.

"The last time I saw my family was back in 1971," he recalled. The youngest of his four children was only six months old when he left. "I think about going back to upper New York to see them, but I don't feel worthy. Maybe it'll happen. I don't know. Look where I'm at, look at what I'm doing." But he stops for a moment and adds, "of course, this is the life I chose."

After high school, Larry enlisted in the navy, where he became a machinist's mate. "My drinking was becoming a problem, but it got worse after I was out of the navy."

In 1966, he married, by that time, "I was drinking every day, but it never showed. After the service, alcohol really had a hold on me. I didn't know it then, but it did." Within a span of five years, he held six different jobs. On one job, he traveled around New England with an expense account, digging foundations for silos. "Giving me that expense account was the worst thing they could have done. I was home only once a month. On the road, I was running up the account on everything except what I should have been using it for," he said. Finally "I got fired because I laid in the house drunk for one week, while the truck stood outside." A few days later, he went to work for a friend at his trucking firm.

In the meantime, he and his family had moved to a 50-acre farm which his parents helped him finance and eventually pay off. His wife had started nursing school.

"All this time, I was drinking like crazy. I'd go for a pizza on a Saturday night, come home hours later, drunk, and without the pizza. I was neglecting my wife and children, all because of drinking." He said that he started "fooling around with women in bars and they would call my house."

Larry's fourth child was born in June 1971, and his wife left in December. "Shortly afterwards, I packed up and went to Florida. I gave up everything."

For the next four or five years, he drank wine and slept in the woods. He said that he was always dirty and smelly, but "I didn't give a damn about nothing." While in Florida, he worked as a day laborer. Once he worked on a shrimp boat, but he made too much money. What he didn't drink, he would throw around. Whenever he wasn't sleeping outside, he would spend the night in flophouses that charged $1.50 a night or $2 with meals.

In 1975, a ride with a sailor brought him to Ohio. He first stayed at the Salvation Army and, shortly afterward, checked into his first alcohol and drug abuse program, sponsored by the Veterans Administration. "Somehow or another, I landed in Pittsburgh, where it was easier to receive welfare," he recalled. While in Pittsburgh, on two separate occasions, he checked himself into the Salvation Army's Drug and Rehabilitation Center.

For the past two years, Larry has stayed at several missions in southeastern Ohio and southwestern Pennsylvania. He pays for his room and board by cooking or performing odd jobs at the missions. One and a half years ago, he contacted his parents for the first time since 1971. They spent a week with him then. He was to see them again this year but went on a drunken spree. He has tried to call his parents collect; but they refuse to accept his calls. His father has told him not to call anymore, because every time the phone rings they expect the worst..

Larry has stopped drinking again. He plans to be moving on soon, probably to another rescue mission, another town, another odd job if he can find one.

While their numbers are small compared to other categories of homeless, there are some true vagabonds who experience the lack of a fixed address not as a form of deprivation but as a rewarding freedom from control and responsibility. In the future, continued expansion and improvement of the emergency food and shelter system might make this an appealing alternative for more such people. However, there is no evidence to suggest that, to date, any substantial proportion of the U.S. homeless population are volunteers for this style of life or that the expansion of shelters has contributed to the increase of homelessness.

Mental illness and substance abuse

The perception that many homeless are either mentally ill or addicted to drugs or alcohol has been supported previously by a number of local studies (some based on a single shelter population) that have found anywhere from one-fourth to a large majority to be mentally ill (Bachrach 1984a). HUD's 1984 survey of shelter operators produced a lower estimate of the rate of mental illness (22 percent); the shelter operators also estimated, on average, that 38 percent of those they served had a problem with alcohol or drugs. Taking into account the probable overlap between the two groups (said to be 10 to 20 percent), and assuming that the "hard-core street population" had a higher incidence of such problems than the shelter occupants, HUD researchers concluded, "it is very probable that a clear majority of the homeless are chronically disabled" (p. 24).

It appears that as many as one-third of the Ohio homeless have had trouble with alcohol or drugs (see the box below). As noted earlier, 30 percent have been hospitalized for mental health reasons (but are not necessarily mentally ill). A significant minority of the homeless in Ohio, in an earlier era, would have remained in institutions for long periods, some indefinitely; so would a larger number of other people who, following their deinstitutionalization, have not become homeless.

SHANE

Shane is an 18-year-old drug addict on parole for robbing a liquor store. Because of his past police record, he was sentenced to 18 months in prison. With help from the director of the local Volunteers of America, he is staying at the agency's shelter rather than in prison.

Shane left home at 17, after a fight with his father. He slept in a boxcar for a few days, stayed at a friend's house for a month, then with another friend in another town near Shane's home. While Shane was living there, the Volunteers' director heard that he was having a hard time of it—"drinking, on drugs, with no money, no place to go, no one to depend on." On the day that the director came to pick him up, his friend robbed a liquor store next door. According to Shane, this friend robbed the store alone and put the stolen goods in the house, then left. Two weeks after the robbery, the police called the Volunteers' director, asking him to bring Shane back to face indictment. Shane remained in jail for 50 days awaiting trial. Finally, the judge put him into the director's custody for three years. He is allowed to visit his parents and fiancée twice every month.

Shane and his twin brother were adopted as two-year-olds. Their new parents had their names legally changed so they could never be found. When, at age 12, Shane learned that he had been adopted, the news triggered a powerful reaction: "I guess I was hurt because that meant my real parents got rid of me." He says he will always be hurt. Shane added, "When we were told about the adoption, my brother accepted it. I rebelled."

Shane's parents put him in a detention home at one point. He does not remember when he started drinking, but does remember that he would pick up his father's beer cans, laying around the house, and drink whatever was left over. At thirteen, he began to use drugs, "just about anything that came around."

The one bright spot in his life has recently brought him a great deal of pain. Shane has known the girl who is now his fiancée since she was twelve years old. Three years later, while he was in prison, his fiancée had a baby, which was put up for adoption. "It brought back thoughts about my adoption. I didn't want my baby to go through what I went through."

Shane believes he is no longer an alcoholic. But, he says that whenever he gets nervous, he gets the "urge," because a beer had always calmed him down in the past.

Looking ahead, Shane's goals are to get out of the shelter, finish high school, get a good job, and get married.

It does not necessarily follow that because many homeless were once institutionalized, the policy of deinstitutionalization is therefore a major underlying cause of homelessness (c.f. Halpern et al. 1980). The reduction in institutional populations was virtually over by 1980; yet the numbers of homeless apparently have risen rapidly since then. Also, the relationship between institutionalization and mental illness is not clear-cut (see the box following). The lack of reliable shelter makes a person more likely than average to be referred for psychological screening, to exhibit bizarre behavior (whether or not it is linked to an underlying psychological disorder), and to willingly accept short-term institutionalization—if only as a source of food and shelter. One piece of evidence that might provide the link between deinstitutionalization and homelessness is the extent to which the homeless are individuals with severe emotional disorders that are controlled only through medication and, in earlier decades, would have almost certainly mandated long-term or permanent hospitalization. Given the importance of this particular question both to mental health professionals and to those concerned with policies for the homeless, it is dealt with at greater length in Chapter 5; for the moment, we will leave the extent to which mental illness, alcohol or drug addiction, or deinstitutionalization policies place people at risk of becoming homeless.

BLONDIE

They call her "Blondie" on the streets, but she said her real name is Nancy. She hangs out on a downtown street she calls "Main Street." Nearby is a soup kitchen that serves a meal every day except Wednesdays, Saturdays, and Sundays. Sundays, Blondie goes to another place that serves meals only on that day. She does not eat on Wednesdays and Saturdays.

Ironically, she says she is on a diet. At St. Vincent DePaul's soup kitchen, she ate the two hot dogs given to her, but left the buns on her plate because, she said, they are fattening.

Blondie is 52 years old but looks older. She is very thin. The teeth she has left are rotted. Her straight blond hair touches her shoulders. She complains of arthritis in her neck and shows how she stays bundled up in the bitter cold of this winter.

Blondie says she was 28 when her "nerves let go." At that time, she spent about six weeks in a state hospital for the mentally ill where, she says, they gave her lemon juice as medicine; then they let her go. She had no income and no family and had lost the house she had occupied before her breakdown. She has not been hospitalized in recent years.

Usually when it gets cold, Blondie rents a room above a downtown tavern for $91 a month. She receives a General Assistance check of $117 a month and $78 in food stamps. But when the weather gets warm she is on the streets again, her checks stop coming because she said she can never get a check when she doesn't have a residence. During the warm months, she carries a bag that contains her things.

When Blondie goes into the welfare office, she "prepares for the worst," because "they are not nice to her." She says "the public" has done barbaric things to her. "There is not one thing they have not done to me."

CONCLUSION

Between those, such as the authors of the New York State report, who see homelessness primarily as institutional failure and those, such as Main, who see it as manifesting individual weakness, there stretches a jumbled landscape of conflicting information and interpretations. Certainly among the homeless there can be found almost "pure" cases to support each argument. However, not every argument is equally consistent with the available data. Taken together, HUD's national survey of shelter operators and the Ohio survey provide the broadest and most reliable basis so far for sorting out, and perhaps partly reconciling, conflicting explanations.

Beginning at a general level, most people become homeless not as a result of a single catastrophic event, but at the end of a series of misfortunes. Homelessness is not a dramatic fall from seemingly secure middle-class life. Most had been poor and on the margin of the labor force prior to becoming homeless. Their present condition reflects not only their inability to earn income by working, but also a social welfare system that provides haphazard and often inadequate coverage of those unable to support themselves. It is striking, given the extremely low rate of employment among this group, that fewer than two in five rely primarily for their current income on public welfare, Social Security, private charity, or personal pensions. Their lack of secure shelter is a by-product of their poverty, combined with isolation from friends and relatives. The battered wife, the youthful runaway, the "higher-functioning" young males on the road by choice—these appear to be exceptions, accounting together for a relatively small proportion of today's homeless.

Still unsettled, however, is the extent to which the poverty and social marginality that characterize the homeless population are products of predisposing personal attributes, specifically, mental illness and alcohol and drug addiction. If a large percentage of the homeless population suffers from chronic severe mental disorder or chemical dependency, then our interpretation of that population's apparent poverty and isolation must be very different. HUD's conclusion that a majority of the homeless suffer at least one of these disabilities, and similar findings from a number of local studies suggest that these may be not only symptoms but causes of homelessness. On the other hand, prior to the Ohio survey, there had been no attempts to directly assess the psychological condition of a broad cross section of the homeless population. In the next chapter, this evidence is brought to bear on the crucial issues of mental illness and deinstitutionalization.

NOTES

1. In a rigorous attempt to categorize the long-term residents of one shelter, one group of researchers could arrive at a clear-cut classification for two out of three only. See Stephen Crystal et al. *Chronic and Situational Dependency: Long-Term Residents in a Shelter for Men* (New York: Human Resources Administration, May 1982).

2. Information obtained from the homeless is not sufficient to assess the extent of their eligibility for various forms of public assistance or the extent to which they actually receive these benefits. The complexity of rules governing eligibility and benefit under AFDC, Food Stamps, and Medicaid has increased in recent years. That complexity, combined with frequent rule changes, makes it difficult for program workers "to explain exactly who may receive welfare and how much they would get in a clear and general way that could inform people's decisions about whether to apply for welfare. Potential applicants must decide for themselves whether they are poor enough to receive welfare" (Bane and Dowling 1985, 9).

3. The impacts of tax policy and other public policies on the housing problems of the poor are complex and often contradictory. See Downs (1983) for a careful discussion of these effects.

—— 5 ——

THE HOMELESS MENTALLY ILL

I see, in this thoroughfare, a natural, followed by children. . . . Consider this unhappy wretch; poor mad fool, what will he do with so many rages and tatters? . . . I have seen wild lunatics shouting insults in the street. . . .

Francois Colletet, quoted in M. Foucault (1965)

To this point, we have taken a broad view of the problem of homelessness in America. In this chapter, however, we focus on the narrower issue of mental illness and the homeless. This topic deserves special attention for two reasons. First, the press, policymakers, advocates, professional researchers, and caregivers have been preoccupied with the prevalence of mental illness among the homeless population. Second, the homeless who are mentally ill have special needs that call for innovative public action.

Some have read the evidence about the incidence of mentally ill and alcohol or drug abuse among the homeless as indicating that most suffer from one or both problems. They have used such evidence to suggest that deinstitutionalization policies make a major contribution to the numbers of homeless and that many are in need of mental health treatment, possibly in a custodial setting, that they are not receiving. Others, such as Levine and Stockdill (1986, 15), have noted that "the number of programs specifically designed to assist those who are both mentally ill and homeless are woefully inadequate in relation to need" and emphasize the need for alternative housing and other forms of community support for this group.

The evidence on which such conclusions are based is far from definitive. Serious conceptual and measurement difficulties stand in the way of firm conclusions about the extent of need or the shortfall of specialized services. However, such

Some of the analyses reported here were originally conducted by Jerry Bean (see ODMH 1985). We gratefully acknowledge his contribution to the project.

difficulties do not prevent some from characterizing the homeless as predominantly composed of the mentally ill and the addicted. The mayor of New York, for example, by inappropriately adding together questionable figures on the proportions of single homeless people in his city's public shelters who are said to be mentally ill, alcoholic, or drug addicted, has suggested that 90 percent have at least one of these problems (PBS, "MacNeil/Lehrer News Hour," December 23, 1985). This conclusion permits him to describe the single mentally ill as "ill people"—a view that supports the involuntary hospitalization of those who want to remain outside on cold nights and which, not incidentally, shifts attention away from the city's housing and urban renewal policies as possible contributors to its large homeless population.

The available evidence does not support such a conclusion. In this chapter, we take a careful look at that evidence and the assumptions and methods it employs. Specifically, the chapter addresses the following questions:

1. What is the most useful way to define, classify, and measure the psychiatric problems of the homeless population?
2. What is the best evidence, based on the Ohio survey and previous research, regarding the incidence of mental illness among the homeless?
3. What is the overlap, among the homeless, between mental illness and alcohol or drug abuse?
4. What is the overlap, among the homeless, between previous hospitalization for mental health reasons and current symptoms of severe psychopathology?

We must begin answering these questions by recognizing how difficult are the conceptual and methodological problems confronting this aspect of research on the homeless.

IDENTIFYING MENTAL ILLNESS

Most Americans probably view homeless people as, in some way, "abnormal." There must be something very wrong with those who dress in rags; rarely bathe; talk to themselves; hurl curses at passersby; sleep in doorways, on subway ventilation grates, or on park benches; eat food from trash dumpsters; and never work. Some community mental health professionals also believe that a high proportion of the homeless are mentally ill, not necessarily for the reasons above but also because these professionals encounter many of the more disturbed homeless in their work (Baxter and Hopper 1982, 397; Bachrach 1984a).

The behavior of the visible homeless encourages the perception that most homeless are somehow disturbed. Life on the streets or in shelters is such that many chronically homeless people appear to be mentally ill when in reality they manifest symptoms reflective of their environment. The homeless who appear paranoid while living on the street or in shelters may be quite realistic in their fear of being robbed, beaten, abused, or killed. Add to this the physiological stresses resulting from poor nutrition, lack of sleep, and exposure, and it is no wonder that many homeless people manifest some psychopathological symptoms (Hauch 1985). Remove these problems and the symptoms may quickly abate (Baxter and Hopper 1982, 402). Many homeless people are shy, often frightened, deliberately unobtrusive, and may lack social skills. The Ohio interviewers observed that homeless people with these characteristics often act strangely, invoking a kind of self-defense mechanism. Several interviewers found that once they developed a rapport with the homeless and demonstrated that they meant them no harm, their behavior transformed into something more closely approaching expected norms or values.

There is other evidence that suggests that the proportion of the homeless who are mentally ill may have been exaggerated. It is important to remember that many homeless people are short-term, one-time-only victims of some special social, economic, or personal circumstance. These include victims of disasters, house evictions, family breakups, job loss, and other misfortune. Restoring a person's pre-crisis circumstances would not only relieve the condition of homelessness, but might also remove symptoms that could be mistaken for severe psychopathology (e.g., losing control when your landlord throws your belongings in the street). Even those who have been homeless for a long time cannot be assumed to be mentally ill. Transients and drifters who have chosen this style of life (see especially Priest 1971, 1976) and those who ordinarily live in cheap lodgings but periodically abandon them in favor of accommodation at a relatively comfortable, free shelter facility (Hauch 1985) may exhibit no symptoms of psychopathology.

The imposition of norms or values of the mental health profession on the homeless, who represent a different subculture, may have led to confusion (Ball 1982; Barrow and Lowell 1982; Segal and Baumohl 1980; Bachrach 1984a; Spradley 1980, 330; Hauch 1985, 7). Also, where clinical diagnosis is impossible and where information must be produced in short interviews or by unobtrusive observation, it is likely that some chronic alcohol or substance abusers will be misclassified as mentally ill and vice versa. While it is true that some substance abusers are mentally ill, the extent of overlap between the two groups is far from complete; yet they may exhibit similar behavior. This being the case, it is often difficult to distinguish among problems (Bachrach 1984a). Finally, classifying homeless people who were once hospitalized in a psychiatric facility as mentally ill because they are now homeless is problematic. Although a history of psychiatric illness may predispose a person to poverty and homelessness, we cannot presume that homelessness is a symptom or consequence of mental illness in every such case.

In short, there is a tendency among observers to interpret as evidence of serious psychopathology behavior that is either an adaptation to the condition of homelessness, a reflection of nonpathological personality or cultural differences between the homeless and their observers, or an indication of other problems.

The more reflective and careful research on this question, of which there is a rapidly growing amount, recognizes these pitfalls. Conceptually, there has been an effort to separate out serious psychopathology from the background noise of sometimes bizarre, possibly disturbed, behavior that does not indicate serious, chronic mental illness. In this regard, we share the views of Leona Bachrach (1984a), who suggests that the focus of the policy debate be not on the mental health services needed by the homeless generally, but rather on how to help persons who are seriously mentally ill, who ordinarily fall within the purview of psychiatry, and who are homeless. These are persons ''whose homelessness is either an expression of their complicated psychopathology or else contributes significantly to the course of that pathology'' (p.3). In her words (p. 140):

> [From a policy formulation perspective, analysis should deal] exclusively with those individuals whose pathology and symptomatology are clearly those of the chronically mentally ill. The definition of chronicity in mental illness has, in fact, undergone considerable change in recent years, so that the chronically mentally ill individual is currently generally regarded as an individual with a major mental disorder ''who needs psychiatric services indefinitely to attain and preserve the maximum possible independence from a substantially disabling mental illness and its consequences'' (Peele and Palmer 1980, 63), irrespective of his/her diagnosis or length of stay in a psychiatric inpatient facility. Severity and persistence of disability and dependency of indefinite duration are thus the distinguishing hallmarks of chronicity in today's essentially noninstitutional system of care (Bachrach 1983).

Following Bachrach, it seems the homeless will be better served by attempting to identify cases that are so severe that psychiatric services are called for. In most instances, these cases will require long-term custodial care or short-term stabilization followed by regular monitoring, whether in an institution or community setting. Those not requiring psychiatric services may be helped first by fulfilling their short-term emergency needs, which may involve some minimal forms of mental health care, and their long-term needs, which may involve one or more of a varied array of social services. A scheme for classifying the homeless on the basis of their service needs will be presented in Chapter 6.

WHAT WE KNOW ABOUT THE HOMELESS MENTALLY ILL

During 1983 and 1984, the National Institute of Mental Health (NIMH) funded a number of research projects on the homeless. As part of this effort, a comprehensive literature review and assessment were undertaken concerning the homeless mentally ill (Bachrach 1984a, 1984b). Some of the major findings are summarized below.

The estimated proportion of the homeless population that suffers from mental illness varies greatly from study to study. Studies conducted in individual cities, usually in a single shelter, and reviewed by Bachrach (1984a) concluded that anywhere from one-fourth (New York State Office of Mental Health 1982) to one-half (Baxter and Hopper 1981; Depp and Ackis 1983) of the homeless were mentally ill. Most estimates, though, fall in the 30 to 40 percent range (Arce et al. 1983; Bassuk 1983; Chmiel et al. 1979; Streltzer 1979; Crystal et al. 1982). An exceptional study of one shelter's occupants showed an incidence of diagnosable mental illness as high as 90 percent (Bassuk 1984, 42). On the other hand, shelter operators surveyed by HUD (U.S. Dept of HUD 1984), on average, estimate the proportions of their residents with major mental health problems to be only about 22 percent. The HUD report suggests that this figure may understate the prevalence of mental illness among the homeless because the incidence of such problems is likely to be higher in the population outside shelters.

A field study of 248 homeless in thirteen St. Louis shelters is typical of the more carefully designed research focused on the incidence of mental illness (Morse et al. 1985). It is of interest because of the fairly extensive sample (although limited to the shelter population in one community), because of the effort to distinguish between "crisis" and "chronic" mental health needs, and because it uses a standard instrument for assessing psychiatric status (the Brief Symptom Inventory). Forty-seven percent of those interviewed "scored above the screening cutoff score which suggests psychiatric disorder" (p. 53). About 20 percent were said to have "chronic mental health need," meaning that they had reported "multiple or lengthy hospitalizations" for mental health reasons; of this group, about two-thirds had "elevated psychiatric symptoms." This study points up two of the major research decisions encountered in such work: (1) whether to rely on past hospitalization as one indication of current mental problems; and (2) what, necessarily arbitrary, cutoff scores to select as a basis for classifying needs. The results of all large-sample studies, since they cannot rely on painstaking clinical diagnoses, are very sensitive to these two choices.

Other researchers have studied the proportion of shelter occupants who have a history of psychiatric care, especially in psychiatric hospitals. Bachrach (1984a), in her review, found that most studies estimated a rate of about one in three (see Arce et al. 1983; Bassuk 1983; Brown et al. 1983; and Tabler 1982). A study of transients seeking Traveler's Aid assistance in San Francisco, however, found six in ten with a history of hospitalization (Lewis 1978).

Several studies have examined the prevalence of alcohol and drug abuse among the homeless. Participants in a 1983 ADAMHA round table estimated that between 10 and 15 percent of the homeless had severe drug abuse problems, while between 40 and 45 percent were chronic alcoholics or had severe problems with drinking (Levine 1984). The HUD (1984) survey of shelter operators indicated that about 38 percent of the sheltered homeless had alcohol and/or drug abuse problems. Most studies have found considerable overlap between the two groups of substance abusers.

When HUD (1984) researchers combined their estimates of the sheltered homeless with mental illness problems and those with alcohol/drug problems (allowing for a 10 to 20 percent overlap between these problems), they concluded that about one-half of the population was affected by one or both problems.

Although research findings about the homeless mentally ill are now beginning to accumulate, our knowledge of this group is still very incomplete. Not only are the homeless mentally ill, like other homeless, difficult to study (see Chapter 2); only recently have social scientists and psychologists given much attention to the connections between homelessness and mental illness. Only since 1983, in fact, has significant funding been provided for such research.

Published research on the homeless and mental illness often has limitations that reduce its potential contribution to the public policy debate. Much of the best work on the homeless mentally ill is done by psychiatrists or psychologists who interview people in depth to develop clinical diagnoses. This procedure requires a highly skilled professional and involves lengthy interviews and often elaborate psychological testing. Such research is problematic mainly because samples tend to be small and taken from controlled settings such as a clinic or shelter; and, as a consequence, its findings are not directly generalizable to the larger homeless population.

Survey research methods, on the other hand, can be used to yield findings of broader generality. This methodology can employ abbreviated psychological instruments or other questions to elicit limited information from a large, representative sample of the homeless population. Unfortunately, survey research cannot develop case-level data that has the same level of certainty as a clinical diagnosis. At best, survey research can produce "ball park" estimates of the proportions of the homeless who have one or a cluster of symptoms. Generalizability is obtained at the expense of certainty.

THE OHIO STUDY

In Ohio, the mental health status of the homeless was assessed using the Psychiatric Status Schedule (PSS) developed by Robert Spitzer and his associates (1970). Ten symptom scales composed of separate items or questions were selected from the much larger set of 321 items comprising the full PSS. Items were weighted in calculating scale scores. The higher the score on each scale, the more severe the symptomatology. (A summary of the definitions, weighting scheme, and scale values are presented in an appendix to this chapter.)

Psychometricians recognize that mental health and mental illness are not exact states such that a person is either healthy or ill. Instead, mental health is assessed on a continuum reflecting better or worse health or more or less illness. Researchers who developed the PSS (see Ohio Department of Mental Health, 1985, for a review) established several levels of psychopathology, as manifested on each scale. On each scale, the range of scores (from 0, indicating no symptoms, to the highest score on the scale) was divided into six levels: no symptoms, minimal, mild, moderate, severe, and extreme severity. These levels have been used in previous work with the PSS (see Ohio Department of Mental Health 1985). Scores ranging from moderate to extreme indicate the likely presence of a severe pathology.

Nine of the ten scales above were combined into two summary indices: one reflecting psychiatric severity and the other behavioral disturbance severity. Index scores calculated by assigning to each scale a value of 1 if the score fell in the moderate to extreme range and a value of 0 if the score ranged from no symptoms to mild, and then summing. The psychiatric index ranged in value from 0 to 4, with 0 indicating no symptomatology on any of the four scales and 4 indicating that a score of moderate to extreme was present on each of the four scales composing the index. The behavioral disturbance index was similarly constructed, using five scales. (The chapter appendix lists the scales used in each index.)[1]

Scores for each index were used to identify possible cases with severe mental disorders, who probably require psychiatric services (Spitzer et al. 1980). Individuals scoring a 3 or 4 on the psychiatric index and a 4 or 5 on the behavioral disturbance index were classified as needing psychiatric services, probably of a custodial nature.

The extent to which psychiatric assessments identify individual psychiatric cases and service needs (that is, the validity of psychological status testing) is at the heart of the issue of mental illness and the homeless. There is considerable disagreement among mental health professionals not only in using assessments to identify psychiatric cases (see Dohrenwend et al. 1978; Spitzer et al. 1980), but also about how such assessments translate into the need for different levels and kinds of psychiatric services (see Bachrach 1984b, 6). This issue has been addressed in two ways. First, the choice of instruments and cutoffs indicating psychiatric severity is based on the interpretations and analyses of Spitzer and his associates (1970, 1980). Although psychiatric cases cannot be firmly established, there is sufficient supporting research to suggest that the instruments and cutoff scores are identifying subpopulations that are probably in need of psychiatric services. These issues are more thoroughly discussed elsewhere (see Ohio Department of Mental Health 1985). Second, the approach used here has been validated by a consensus of expert interpretation. Five Ph.D. researchers experienced in conducting research with or interpreting survey results from the PSS examined the procedures and analyses. They concluded that this methodology would identify probable or likely psychiatric cases among the Ohio homeless. The methodology, having yielded a consensus among practitioners, thus may be said to have content validity (see Jensen 1980, 297).

Examination of the distribution of responses on each component scale of the PSS also tends to confirm their validity. It is of interest to note that "the shape of almost all of these distributions matches the type of distribution one would expect to find in the measurement of psychiatric symptomatology (ODMH 1985, 110). Psychiatric symptoms are rare phenomena, especially in general populations, so that distributions have a J, or positively skewed, shape with most respondents having no or few symptoms and an increasingly smaller number showing higher-symptom levels. The distribution of responses by the Ohio homeless to these scales shows just such a pattern, except in the case of the Depression-Anxiety scale. These distributions "stand in contrast to the picture presented by the popular literature about homelessness and by some researchers who have reported on the prevalence of mental illness among homeless people" (ODMH 1985, 110).

Prevalence of mental disorder

Although most previous studies have estimated the rate of severe mental disorder or chronic mental illness among the homeless population at 25 to 50 percent, the Ohio findings indicate a lower prevalence. In Ohio (see Figure 5.1), 69 percent of the homeless have no self-reported psychopathologies on the psychiatric severity index, and 46 percent have no psychopathology on the behavioral disturbance index. About 36 percent of the Ohio homeless had zero scores on both indices. They can be considered relatively symptom-free. Another one-third have at least one behavioral disturbance problem but no indication of a psychiatric problem. These are people who may behave in odd or deviant ways but do not demonstrate any need for psychiatric services. The remaining homeless demonstrate the presence of at least one psychiatric problem.

If we assume that severe mental disorders are represented by those scoring at least a 4 on the behavioral disturbance severity index or at least a 3 on the psychiatric severity index, then only 10 percent of the homeless in Ohio who are affected are in this category (see Table 5.1). Given the skewed distribution of scores on these indices, the estimate of the rate of severe illness is not highly sensitive to the choice of cutoff scores. However, if we were to assume that those scoring above 3 or 2, respectively, on the two indices are at risk of lapsing into severe levels of psychopathology or are borderline chronic mentally ill, then another 8 percent would be added, making the total affected or at risk of severe mental illness 18 percent. Even with this less restrictive level of severity, the Ohio results do not reach the prevalence rates for mental disorders found in other studies of shelter populations or broader samples of the homeless. In fact, in order to obtain the prevalence rates found in some individual shelter studies, it would be necessary to include all those scoring at least 2 on both the behavioral disturbance and psychiatric symptom indices, which would yield a rate of about 40 percent.[2]

FIGURE 5.1.   Ohio homeless psychiatric and behavioral disturbance severity indices (percentages)

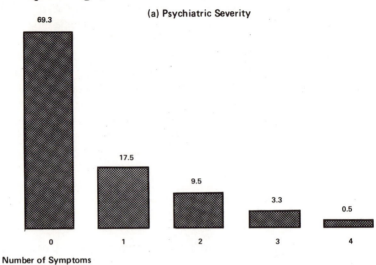

Source: Ohio Department of Mental Health, 1985.

Symptoms of mental disorder

Previous research has identified a variety of symptoms of mental disorder among the homeless (see Bachrach 1984a). When the nine-symptom subscales forming the psychiatric and behavioral disturbance severity indices are looked at separately, the patterns are revealing (see Figure 5.2).

TABLE 5.1. Overlapping psychiatric and behavioral disturbance problems: Moderate and above

Number of psychiatric symptoms	Number of behavioral disturbance symptoms						
	0	1	2	3	4	5	Total
0	36.2	15.6	8.0	6.0	2.9	0.5	69.2
1	6.6	4.5	3.4	1.8	0.8	0.3	17.5
2	2.9	2.5	1.7	1.1	0.9	0.4	9.5
3	0.6	0.5	1.0	0.8	0.3	0.1	3.3
4	0.0	0.0	0.2	0.0	0.2	0.1	0.5
Total	46.3	23.1	14.3	9.7	5.1	1.4	100.0

Source: Ohio Department of Mental Health 1985, 114.

The most severe levels of possible psychopathology are found on those scales associated with behavioral disturbance and not on those associated with psychiatric severity. The three most prevalent sets of symptoms are speech disorganization; inappropriate affect, behavior, or appearance; and retardation (not mental retardation) or lack of emotion. The fifth and sixth most frequently observed symptoms (only slightly less prevalent) are agitation or excitement followed by disorientation or memory impairment. Only two psychiatric measures, suspicion/persecution/hallucination, and depression/anxiety, occur at fourth and fifth position in degree of prevalence.

These patterns suggest a potential problem in labeling as chronic mentally ill those exhibiting deviant behaviors on the street or in shelters. According to mental health professionals who have used the PSS extensively, the psychiatric index tends to highlight mental disorders, while the behavioral disturbance index may pick up not only psychopathology, but also behaviors not necessarily related to mental illness (ODMH 1985). So, for example, few would argue that hallucinations (a scale included in the psychiatric index) are normal occurrences. But, "general lack of emotional expression" (Spitzer et al. 1970, 44), which could be evidence of some severe pathology at work, might also constitute an expected and perhaps appropriate reaction to the reality of life on the street or in shelters. Although we do not wish to overextend our conclusions, it is possible that estimates of chronic mental disorder among the homeless based on casual observation (whether by a shelter operator or a mental health professional), rather than clinical testing and diagnosis, tend to deduce illness from behavior that is quite appropriate for the extreme circumstances under which the homeless live (see especially Hauch 1985).

Comparisons with two studies support the above interpretation. In one study, Spitzer and his colleagues (1970) examined 770 newly admitted psychiatric inpatients; and in another study, researchers associated with the Ohio Department

FIGURE 5.2. Ohio homeless symptom scale score distributions

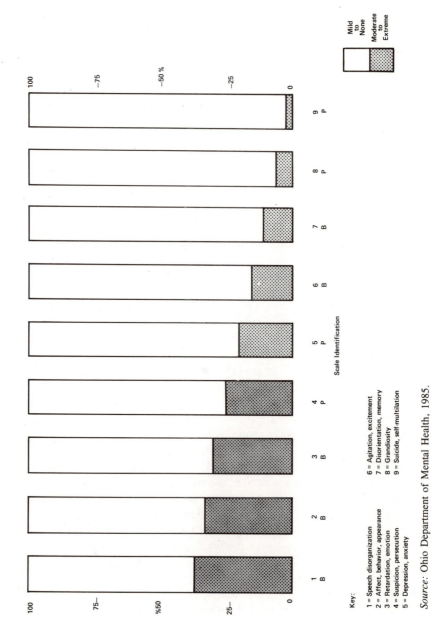

Key:

1 = Speech disorganization
2 = Affect, behavior, appearance
3 = Retardation, emotion
4 = Suspicion, persecution
5 = Depression, anxiety

6 = Agitation, excitement
7 = Disorientation, memory
8 = Grandiosity
9 = Suicide, self-mutilation

Source: Ohio Department of Mental Health, 1985.

of Mental Health (see ODMH 1985, 116–117) examined 229 people who had once been hospitalized in a psychiatric facility and at the time of the study were *successfully* living in the community. Both studies used the PSS instrument.

Using a standard statistical technique,[3] homeless people in Ohio were compared to respondents in the other studies (see ODMH 1985). Figures 5.3 and 5.4 show the comparison between the Ohio homeless and the Spitzer (1970) and Ohio Department of Mental Health (1985) studies, respectively. The dotted lines indicate scores of the two comparison groups, while the solid lines represent the Ohio homeless. If the dotted and solid lines coincided, this would indicate that the homeless and the comparison groups have identical scores. Where the solid line falls to the right of the dotted line, homeless people show worse symptoms than the comparison group. Conversely, where the solid line falls to the left, the homeless people show fewer symptoms.

Both figures suggest that the Ohio homeless population includes a higher proportion of those with severe behavioral disturbance than do the comparison groups but is, at the same time, either better off or no worse off in terms of psychiatric severity (represented by the subjective distress and reality testing scales).

These results could lead to different, and perhaps competing, conclusions. One possible conclusion supports our suggestion that homelessness causes peo-

FIGURE 5.3. Ohio homeless and new-admitted inpatients compared

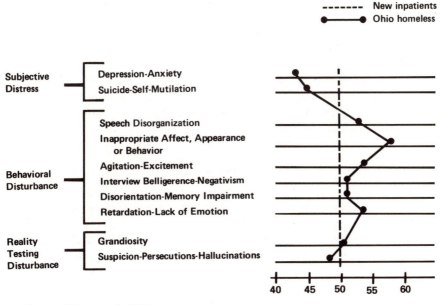

Source: Spitzer, et al. 1970.

FIGURE 5.4. Ohio homeless and Ohio transitional service clients

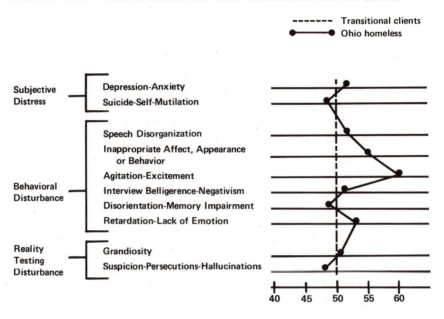

Source: Ohio Department of Mental Health 1985.

ple to behave in strange ways, but in ways that are appropriate for life on the street or in shelters. Their bizarre behavior probably does not indicate, in many cases, a need for psychiatric services. The other possibility is that the severity of behavioral symptoms among Ohio's homeless indicates a population, many of whom have low level disorders or are at risk of developing severe disorders, either due to the stresses of being homeless or for independent reasons. In either case, it is behavioral disturbance rather than psychiatric disorder that manifests itself most strongly.

Variations within the homeless population

Whatever the general incidence of behavioral disturbance and psychiatric disorder among the homeless, it can be expected to vary depending on the severity of deprivation (source of shelter and duration) and other factors associated with the causes of mental illness. For example, the stresses of living on the street may yield a higher incidence of dysfunction among this group than among those in shelters. Similarly, it is reasonable to expect that both street and shelter people will be worse off, on average, than those homeless with other temporary accommodations. These differences may explain, in part, the lower levels of psychopathology observed in Ohio's homeless population than in other studies: the Ohio study included a broad definition of homelessness, while nearly every other study focused on shelter population. Those "on the street" have a significantly higher rate of behavioral disturbance than those in shelters or in other temporary accommodations; but the three groups have very similar average scores on the index of psychiatric severity. Thus, taking into account the differences in defining homelessness, the Ohio results still show a lower prevalence of mental illness than reported in clinical studies and surveys of less extensive samples.

The relationship between duration of homelessness and psychological status also is less straightforward than anticipated (Table 5.2). Those who have been homeless for longer than a year report more symptoms than others on the psychiatric severity index. However, on the index of behavioral disorder, both those who have been homeless for more than a year and those homeless for less than a week score significantly higher than the intermediate groups. Such mixed evidence adds further complexity to the picture of psychopathology among the homeless.

Demographics

Other researchers have noted differences in mental health status among the homeless that are related to sex, race, and age. "Like the chronically mentally ill in general (Goldman et al. 1981), these individuals [i.e., homeless] do not constitute a uniform population either diagnostically, demographically, functionally, or in terms of their residential histories" (Bachrach 1984a, 149). In the Ohio

TABLE 5.2. Level of homelessness, duration, and symptomatology

	Psychiatric			Behavioral		
	Mean	F	Sign.	Mean	F	Sign.
Level of homelessness						
Street	.53	0.83	.436	1.52	9.46	.000
Shelter	.48			0.98		
Other	.42			1.10		
Temporary						
Duration of homelessness (days)						
1–7	.42	2.49	.030	1.31	4.04	.001
8–30	.43			0.97		
31–90	.45			0.90		
91–180	.37			0.88		
181–365	.61			0.99		
365+	1.11			1.33		

Source: Ohio Department of Mental Health 1985.

sample, no significant differences in symptom rates were observed to be related to age. This finding contrasts with that of a Boston area survey of the homeless that found that those with high scores on a mental illness symptoms scale averaged 31 years of age (versus an average age of 38 for the whole sample), and that three-quarters were under 35 (Human Services Research Institute 1985). Nor were significant differences observed between males and females or between minority and nonminority homeless on the psychiatric severity index. However, blacks scored much higher than whites, and males scored higher than females on the index of behavioral disturbance (see Table 5.3). Similarly, the homeless in urban areas (who are more likely to be minority and female) exhibit rates of psychiatric symptoms similar to the rural homeless but show higher rates of behavioral disturbance. Once again, this pattern could suggest either a protective adaptation to a hostile environment or low level disorders produced by the stresses of homelessness or otherwise.

Hospitalization and deinstitutionalization

The major shift, since the 1950s, away from long-term hospitalization of the mentally ill is viewed by some as a major cause of the increase in numbers of homeless in the 1980s (Baxter and Hopper 1982; Lamb 1982b). If true, this view

TABLE 5.3. Demographics and symptomatology

Demographics	Psychiatric			Behavioral		
	Mean	F	Sign.	Mean	F	Sign.
Race						
Whites	.52	2.26	.080	.94	11.75	.000
Blacks	.43			1.36		
Age (years)						
18–29	.50	1.66	.158	.93	2.27	.060
30–39	.49			1.21		
40–49	.55			1.04		
50–59	.43			1.22		
60+	.25			1.02		
Sex						
Male	.46	2.18	.140	1.20	30.91	.000
Female	.56			0.62		
Urbanization						
Urban	.48	0.30	.582	1.20	33.69	.000
Rural	.51			0.60		

Source: Ohio Department of Mental Health 1985.

would mean that a high proportion of the homeless either have been hospitalized for mental illness or are at present seriously ill. However, it has already been pointed out in Chapter 4 that the timing of this policy change does not coincide with the more recent surge in numbers of homeless. And, we have seen that perhaps 10 percent of the homeless in Ohio have symptoms consistent with the presence of severe, chronic disabling mental illness. Such evidence casts doubt on the extent to which the growth of homelessness is attributable to the deinstitutionalization. On the other hand, about 30 percent of the Ohio homeless have been hospitalized at least once for reasons related to mental health. The evidence on hospitalization thus is more consistent with the deinstitutionalization hypothesis than the evidence on current illness.

It is of interest to see how these two measures of mental health need correlate with each other. In the Ohio sample, those who were once hospitalized are far more likely than others to score high on the psychiatric severity index; but they are not different from other homeless in their rate of behavioral disturbance (see Table 5.4).[4] This finding tends to further validate use of the PSS scales to measure need for mental health services. It also confirms the need to distinguish between bizarre behavior and the presence of serious illness, especially when studying the homeless.

TABLE 5.4. Hospitalization, alcohol and drug usage, and symptomatology

	Psychiatric			Behavioral		
	Mean	F	Sign.	Mean	F	Sign.
Psychiatric hospitalization						
Yes	.92	126.32	.000	1.18	3.09	.080
No	.30			1.02		
Use Hospital ER						
Yes	.75	33.79	.000	1.05	.655	.200
No	00			00		
Alcohol consumption						
A lot	.70			1.46		
Some	.38	10.33	.000	1.00	9.83	.000
Not at all	.50			.99		
Drug use						
Yes	.72	39.73	.000	.94	5.72	.020
No	.37			1.15		

Source: Ohio Department of Mental Health 1985.

Most important, the evidence indicates that prior hospitalization, by itself, is an unreliable indicator of present mental health. In most cases, either the severe illness that led to hospitalization has abated or hospitalization occurred, although no illness was present, possibly for short-term observation and clinical testing. Also, because today many more people diagnosed as needing treatment are not institutionalized but rather diverted into community-based care, they may not have a history of hospitalization even though chronically ill. Thus, inferring the extent of need among the homeless for treatment of chronic mental illness from information on the history of hospitalization is inappropriate.

Alcohol and drug abuse

The Ohio study was consistent with previous research on substance abuse among groups in the homeless population. About one-third of the Ohio homeless experienced problems with alcohol and/or drug abuse, a figure falling between other estimates, which fix the rate of prevalence at between 20 to 40 percent on average (see Roth and Bean, 1985, for a discussion of these findings).

Concern about the links between homelessness and the abuse of alcohol is longstanding, but much work still needs to be done on the linkage between these two problems (Whittman 1985). More recently, the spread of other forms of substance abuse has expanded this concern (Reich and Siegel 1978; Baxter and Hopper 1982). Careful research has distinguished these problems from mental illness, but the two problems have tended to merge in popular treatments of the homeless and, as noted earlier, in statements by some public officials.

Evidence from the Ohio survey suggests a moderate correlation between both alcohol and drug abuse, on one hand, and the symptoms of severe psychiatric disorder on the other hand (see Table 5.4). Those with high scores (3 or 4) on this index are more likely than other homeless people to report "a lot" of alcohol consumption. Similarly, those with high index scores are more likely than those with lower scores to report trouble with drugs.

The relationships between substance abuse and behavioral disturbance are not so consistent, however. Those who report high alcohol consumption also are more likely to exhibit symptoms of disturbed behavior. However, those with drug problems actually show less evidence of behavioral disorder. This might indicate a failure on the part of this set of scales to identify abnormal behavioral patterns associated with drug abuse, or it could have other meanings.

In any case, the extensive and not unexpected overlap of substance abuse and chronic mental disorder, among the homeless population, is confirmed and must be taken into account when calculating the combined proportion of the homeless who have one or both problems.

CONCLUSIONS

Some observers of the homeless have, intentionally or unintentionally, overstated the extent to which this population is composed of the mentally ill and of people with alcohol or drug problems. Some research, based on constricted samples or employing very inclusive criteria of mental health needs, has given support and legitimacy to the view that most of the homeless are "ill." However, most research estimates that between 25 and 50 percent are mentally ill; and the Ohio survey suggests that the proportion may be smaller. Nevertheless, there can be no doubt that mental illness, alcoholism, or drug problems are part of the causal sequences that produce many cases of homelessness and, more important, are problems that must be addressed in attempting to reverse that process.

Constructing appropriate public policies for the homeless depends on our ability to make distinctions of need within that population. Most of those who exhibit bizarre behavior may not need prolonged periods of psychiatric medication, counseling, or psychotherapy, much less permanent custodial care. Most of those with a history of institutionalization are not presently in need of treatment for psychiatric disturbance. Alcohol and drug therapy is needed by many who do not have other psychological problems. Those and other distinctions can be useful in assessing the extent of needs for mental health and other services.

Many of the seemingly ill homeless would benefit more from services aimed at achieving stable housing, employment, and income than from treatment focused on psychiatric problems. This is not to say that most of those homeless who do suffer from chronic, severe psychopathology receive appropriate treatment. The Ohio study and other research indicate that a high proportion do not. While only a small proportion may need in-patient care, many others could benefit from out-patient care or day treatment and short-term medication (cf. Human Services Research Institute 1985). The apparent shortfall of services appropriate to the needs of the mentally ill homeless is part of a larger pattern, to which attention now turns: how we can best categorize the varied needs of the homeless, how well are these needs met by the current system of programs and services, and what alternatives to the present system are likely to be both beneficial and practical?

NOTES

1. The two severity indices, psychiatric and behavioral, were defined based on the domain relatedness of the symptom scales according to Spitzer et al. (1970, 44). For example, the Psychiatric Severity Index is composed of the Depression-Anxiety, Suicide-Self-Mutilation, Grandiosity, and Suspicion-Persecution-Hallucinations symptom scales. These scales relate to subjective distress and

reality testing, respectively. The Behavioral Disturbance Severity Index, on the other hand, is composed of Agitation-Excitement, Disorientation-Memory Impairment, Inappropriate Affect, Appearance of Behavior, Speech Disorganization, and Retardation-Lack of Emotion symptom scales. A tenth scale, Interview Belligerence, is not used in the indices. Further justification for combining these symptom scales into simple indices came from two sources. First, Spitzer et al. (1980) reported that three of the scales included in the psychiatric severity index (Suspicion-Persecutions-Hallucination, Depression-Anxiety, and Suicide-Self-Mutilation) discriminated between a group of outpatients and a community sample (point biserial correlations were .45, .53, and .34, respectively). These correlations indicate that respondents who were mental health clients tended to have higher scores on these symptom scales than those respondents who were not clients. A second justification for combining symptom scales comes from a finding in the Ohio study that replicates the Spitzer et al. data. Three of the subscales that Spitzer et al. found to be related to the use of mental health services also tend to be related to the hospitalization experience of the Ohio homeless. The pattern of correlations indicates that homeless people who reported having had one or more hospitalizations for mental health problems also tend to have higher scores on the Depression-Anxiety, Suicide-Self-Mutilation, Grandiosity, and Suspicion-Persecution-Hallucinations symptom scales (ODMH 1985). The implications of this pattern are discussed further in the text.

2. The Ohio Department of Mental Health report (1985) itself indicates that "less than five percent [of the homeless people surveyed] might be candidates for highly structured, protective settings" (p. 113).

3. Means and standard deviations from samples of psychiatric inpatients (Spitzer et al. 1970) and transitional service clients in Ohio were used to convert scores for the homeless into t-scores. This analysis was prepared by Jerry Bean of the Ohio Department of Mental Health.

4. Similarly, the homeless in urban areas—who are more likely to be minority and female— exhibit rates of psychiatric symptoms similar to the rural homeless but show higher rates of behavioral disturbance. Once again, this pattern could suggest either a protective adaptation to a hostile environment or borderline disorders produced by the stresses of homelessness or otherwise.

APPENDIX: Overview of Scales and Items

Scale name	Scale description	Scale range/ No. of Items	Weighted	Index*
Depression/ anxiety	Depression, anxiousness, psychophysiological dysfunctions	0 to 38/38	No	P
Suicide/self-mutilation	Suicide thoughts or attempts; self-mutilation	0 to 7/7	No	P
Speech disorganization	Speech impairment not resulting from physical disability	0 to 29/13	Yes	B
Inappropriate affect, appearance or behavior	Behaviors or acts considered inappropriate by average person	0 to 19/10	Yes	B
Belligerence/ negativism	Uncooperative, sarcastic argumentative	0 to 21/16	Yes	B
Disorientation/ memory impairment	Disorientation to space, time, people	0 to 26/11	Yes	B
Retardation/lack of emotion	Indifferent to surrounding (does not refer to mental retardation)	0 to 22/15	Yes	B
Agitation/ excitement	Pacing, hyperactivity, speech	0 to 7/7	No	B
Grandiosity	Delusions of grandeur, excessive boasting, sensationalism	0 to 12/6	Yes	P
Suspicion/ persecution/ hallucination	Paranoia, delusions, distrustful	0 to 44/18	Yes	P

*P, psychiatric; B, behavioral disturbance.
Source: Spitzer et al. (1970, 44–45).

—— 6 ——

A DIFFERENT PERSPECTIVE

As important as it is to determine who the homeless are and how they came to that condition, it is at least as important, from a public policy standpoint, to assess their present needs. To establish what the homeless need requires a different perspective on their characteristics and personal histories. The focus on their needs leads to questions about the goals of public policies for the homeless, that is, about how their needs can best be met.

SHELTER AND OTHER NEEDS

We cannot discuss needs without, implicitly or explicitly, taking some position on the goals of policy. For instance, the goal may be simply to provide temporary emergency overnight shelter, and perhaps a meal, for those who otherwise would be on the street. This seems, in fact, to be the implicit goal of many current public efforts to aid the homeless, at all levels of government. Or, the goal may be full reintegration with the society, along with full economic self-sufficiency, for as many homeless people as possible. If the former goal is all we have in mind, then we need concern ourselves primarily with the fact some of the homeless lack access to shelters. If something like the latter goal is accepted for consideration, then our concern must be with a broader range of needs.

It has been demonstrated in the preceding chapters that the lack of reliable shelter is often only one of the forms of severe deprivation experienced by this group. If we take the position that homelessness is a severe form of deprivation and thus a condition not to be accepted or passively tolerated as being "normal," then there seems to be no reason why we should not take a similar position regarding other forms of deprivation suffered by the same group. Homelessness is, after all, only a secondary aspect or symptom, in many cases, of poverty and social isolation. This leads to a consideration of what it would take, in various cases, to make the homeless economically secure and provide them with a stable set of connections to other people.

To understand what this broader goal implies for different groups of homeless, we must look at them from a fresh perspective. This exercise will demonstrate that the actions required depend on the particular needs of the individual homeless person. Although survey responses do not provide the basis for diagnosis of individual needs, they are sufficient to establish the approximate proportions of a homeless population that needs particular kinds of help.

A NEED HIERARCHY

There are three groups of homeless whose needs for assistance clearly go beyond the need for temporary, emergency shelter. First, there are people who are unlikely ever to fend successfully for themselves outside a protected environment. They need permanent custodial care. Second, there are homeless who have been unable to achieve economic self-sufficiency because of a major deficit (such as illiteracy) or chronic problem (such as alcoholism) with which they cannot cope unaided. They need assistance that will enable them to overcome these limitations before they can live successfully on their own. Third, there are individuals or families in crisis for a variety of reasons. In most cases, they will be capable of returning fairly soon to a more normal situation but need short-term crisis care, including counseling and other personal and sometimes financial support. Finally, there are homeless people with none of the above needs but who nevertheless need a temporary place to stay. The four groups form a hierarchy, ranging from those who will never return to independent residence to those who can do so without any special assistance.

The classification of homeless people on the basis of their needs for various forms of assistance can be very useful for public policy development and program evaluation. The utility of such a classification will become apparent when the Ohio homeless are grouped on this basis.

Need for permanent custodial care

Three of ten homeless people in Ohio cannot reasonably be expected to sustain independent residence over a long period. If they are not merely to survive but are to be reasonably assured of meeting their needs for shelter, food, health care, and emotional support, then they must live in or be closely attached to an institution or agency dedicated to seeing that their needs are met. These include people whose age and employment history indicate that they have passed permanently out of the labor force, those who are physically disabled, and those with chronic, severe psychological disorders.

About one-half of this first need group are people older than 50 who have not worked for at least three years. As they approach old age, the chances that they can once again sustain themselves outside a congregate or communal setting are likely to diminish in the face of physical deterioration and further isolation from old friends or relatives.

About 8 percent of the Ohio homeless (as estimated in Chapter 5) have emotional disorders of a nature that will require continuing, frequent contact with mental health professionals, either in a hospital or community setting.

And, another 7 percent of the homeless are not otherwise in need of custodial care but have self-diagnosed physical disabilities that prevent them from working. While most physically disabled people in the society are capable of independent living, it is assumed that a high proportion of those physically disabled who have become homeless are among the minority of disabled who will do well only in a protected situation. If this judgment is wrong, then many of the disabled homeless belong in the next category of need.

Need for developmental assistance

About one in four homeless people in Ohio do not need permanent custodial care but have identifiable deficits or remediable problems that must be dealt with before they can be judged likely to live successfully on their own. These include the homeless who have had serious problems with alcohol or drugs, those who have never worked, those with little formal education, and those who, while not severely ill, have been in and out of institutions on a regular basis.

The largest group of homeless in this category (about one-eighth of all homeless) are those who say either that drugs or alcohol caused them trouble in the last month, that they have been drinking "a lot," or that they are homeless because they abuse alcohol or drugs. It is assumed that most of these will continue to have such problems without effective professional intervention. Even if therapy is provided, the proportion who are successfully treated may be low and the cost of each success high; but, without treatment, there is little chance that many in this group will be able to sustain an independent life.

A second group of those needing development assistance are those who have never worked or who have less than a ninth-grade education. In the competition for jobs, those with no work experience or little education are not likely to fare well. It is hard to imagine that, without remedial help of some kind, this group of homeless can achieve economic independence.

Finally, a very small number of homeless who are not diagnosed as having severe chronic disorders nevertheless have been hospitalized three or more times for mental health problems. While the most recent professional judgment may have been that they are capable of independent living, their histories suggest that they may fail without some form of special assistance.

Need for crisis care only

One in five Ohio homeless does not have any apparent need for long-term custodial care, or any major deficit such as those discussed above, but is demonstrably in crisis. These are people who have been homeless for relatively short periods and whose lack of permanent shelter is linked to family conflict or dissolution, an eviction or natural disaster, or being fired or laid off from their most recent jobs. This category includes the highest proportion of women.

About one in ten homeless was evicted from his or her previous residence or left because he or she could not pay the rent, has been homeless less than one year, and does not have any of the problems that suggest a need for custodial care or developmental assistance. In addition, a small number of families and individuals are homeless due to fire or natural disaster. Many may need nothing more than help in locating new affordable housing; others may be waiting to become eligible for housing subsidies or other forms of public assistance.

Another group, nearly as large, are homeless due to conflict within their family or recent separation. They are likely to need crisis counseling, legal aid, or other forms of short-term help in addition to shelter.

Finally, in about one case out of fifty, the precipitating cause of homelessness appears to be recent involuntary job loss due to a plant closing, layoff, or firing, and there is no indication of other needs requiring developmental aid or custodial care. Most in this group can be expected to find new employment without extensive assistance, bringing an end to their homelessness. Some may require extensive retraining, in which case they would be more properly classified with those needing developmental assistance.

Need for shelter only

In addition to those homeless with identifiable needs for assistance other than emergency shelter, there remains a residual group (about one in five in Ohio) whose only apparent need is for shelter, or shelter coupled with emergency food and medical care in some instances. That is, they do not appear to need a permanent protected living arrangement; they have no obvious deficit or problem requiring developmental services; they are not homeless due to some recent or ongoing crisis; and yet they are homeless (Figure 6.1).

This group includes people who simply lack enough income to purchase permanent lodgings. It includes those on the move in search of work. It includes those who prefer to keep moving. And, it presumably includes those who properly belong in the other need categories but whose need for other forms of assistance is not so obvious.

Recognizing that there is considerable room for argument about the definitions and measures used, some needs classification similar to this one is a prereq-

FIGURE 6.1. Approximate proportions of the homeless assigned to four need categories

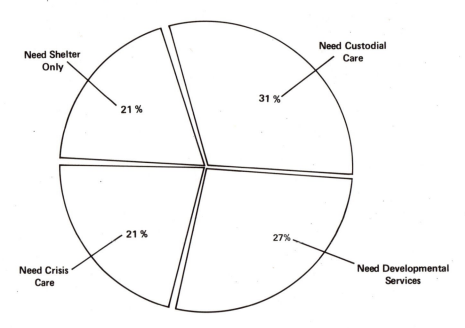

Source: Ohio Department of Mental Health 1985.

uisite for evaluation of current programs to aid the homeless and of alternative policies for this group.[1] To better appreciate how it can be used for decision making and to evaluate the typology itself, it is useful to compare the characteristics of these four groups of homeless.

FOUR NEED GROUPS

When compared to the other three groups of homeless, those who are classified as needing permanent custodial care are distinctive not only in age and mental health status, but in other respects as well (see Table 6.1). Many are in poor health, for instance, being far more likely than other homeless to say they have a medical problem requiring the attention of a doctor. They are more than four times as likely as those in any other group to say that their last job ended for medical reasons. They also are more likely than others to be taking prescribed medicines and more likely to have been hospitalized for mental health reasons.

TABLE 6.1. Selected characteristics of the four need groups

Characteristics	Group needs				
	Custodial care (n = 294)	Developmental aid (n = 252)	Crisis care (n = 196)	Shelter only (n = 198)	All groups (n = 940)
Age					
Under 30	16.6%	32.0%	57.1%	44.4%	35.2%
30–39	15.6	36.4	28.6	33.3	27.7
40–49	12.1	24.8	12.2	18.2	16.8
50–59	35.3	6.0	2.0	3.5	13.7
60+	20.4	0.8	0.0	0.5	6.7
Marital status					
Married; living together	5.2	10.8	16.3	17.3	11.6
Separated	12.7	15.3	17.9	6.6	13.2
Divorced	32.0	26.9	17.9	24.4	26.1
Never married	39.9	43.8	46.4	51.3	44.7
Widowed	10.3	3.2	1.5	0.5	4.5
Education					
0–8 yrs.	29.1	32.2	0.0	0.0	17.7
9–11 yrs.	33.2	28.2	50.0	41.4	37.1
High school grad.	24.6	26.2	36.2	38.9	30.5
Some college	10.0	11.9	12.8	17.2	12.6
College graduate	3.1	1.6	1.0	2.5	2.1
Employment					
Worked in last mo.	16.4	21.3	28.1	41.9	25.5

TABLE 6.1. (Continued)

Characteristics	Group needs				
	Custodial care (n = 294)	Developmental aid (n = 252)	Crisis care (n = 196)	Shelter only (n = 198)	All groups (n = 940)
Ever worked[a]	88.2	67.3	100.0	100.0	86.6
Reason last job ended[b]					
Temporary	13.0	15.8	17.1	24.8	16.8
Closing	7.7	12.0	16.4	4.4	10.1
Fired	12.0	22.6	18.6	8.9	15.3
Quit	16.8	14.3	19.3	21.2	17.7
Poor health	21.6	1.5	2.9	5.3	9.6
Alcohol/drugs	6.7	11.3	0.0	3.5	5.6
Poor mental health	3.4	3.0	0.7	6.2	3.2
All other	18.8	19.6	25.0	25.7	21.7
Primary income source[c]					
Earnings	15.8	23.2	31.2	50.0	27.5
Welfare; charity	30.2	45.0	56.5	26.8	39.3
Family; friends	2.0	4.6	2.2	4.5	3.2
Social security; pension	45.6	16.6	2.2	10.7	21.9
Other; refused	6.5	10.6	8.0	8.0	8.1
No income last mo.	30.5	39.6	29.6	43.4	35.5
Medical					
Need to see doctor	45.1	27.9	20.9	24.9	31.1

Taking drugs; medication prescribed[d]	84.3	60.2	71.7	58.0	70.2
Have been hospitalized for mental health problems	43.8	39.7	13.4	19.3	31.1
Have been in jail or prison	68.8	65.7	38.0	60.1	59.7
In last month, have used: shelters,	61.0	57.2	49.0	62.1	57.7
community mental health centers,	13.8	17.2	8.7	9.1	12.7
community kitchens,	70.3	65.7	44.6	57.6	61.0
hospital emergency rooms,	31.7	25.1	19.9	20.9	25.2
welfare or general relief	37.0	46.2	59.5	44.7	45.8
Can count on relative(s)	32.4	34.9	40.5	43.4	37.1
Can count on friend(s)	34.5	37.4	51.0	49.8	42.0
Length of time in county					
Less than 1 week	15.2	21.4	9.0	21.7	17.2
1 week–1 mo.	15.2	21.4	15.3	31.8	20.7
1–6 mos.	7.6	17.5	18.0	14.7	14.0

TABLE 6.1. (Continued)

	Group needs				
Characteristics	Custodial care (n = 294)	Developmental aid (n = 252)	Crisis care (n = 196)	Shelter only (n = 198)	All groups (n = 940)
6 mos.–1 year	4.7	10.4	11.7	6.2	8.0
Over 1 year	57.3	29.2	46.0	25.6	40.2
Level of homelessness					
Irregular; no shelter	18.2	13.4	14.0	9.8	14.3
Mission; shelter	65.4	60.7	50.3	64.3	60.7
Temporary arrangements	16.4	25.9	35.8	25.9	25.1

[a]Asked of those who did not work in last month.
[b]Asked of those not working but who have worked in the past.
[c]Asked of those who reported some income in preceding month.
[d]Asked of those taking drugs or medication.
Source: Ohio Department of Mental Health 1985.

Nearly one-third have been in a hospital emergency room within the month, compared to one-fourth or less of those in the other need categories. The weight of evidence from the Ohio survey suggests that a high proportion of this group would be physically unable to support themselves through earnings.

Compared to the other need groups, those identified as requiring custodial living arrangements are less likely to have substantial earnings, are relatively isolated from relatives and friends, and are less mobile. Only 16 percent cite earnings as their primary source of income; and three-fourths of those with any income rely mainly on Social Security or pensions (46 percent) or on public welfare or charity (30 percent). Nearly one-third have no current income, which is close to the average for all groups. Over one-half of this group have been in the same county for over a year (not surprising in another population with this age and health profile), but making them less mobile than other homeless. Finally, 25 percent of those in need of custodial care have been homeless for over two years, a proportion that exceeds that of the other three groups. In general, the comparison with other need groups confirms the judgment that this group has been properly classified as being in need of long-term or permanent custodial care.

The second need group, those who are said to need developmental services, is not particularly distinctive on any demographic or behavioral dimension, with the obvious exceptions of their relative lack of education and more frequent involvement with alcohol or drugs. One in three has completed fewer than nine years of school. One-third of those not now employed have never worked. Eleven percent of those not currently working but who worked in the past say they lost their last jobs due to drinking or drug problems, and another 22 percent were fired for unspecified reasons. Also, those needing developmental assistance are less likely than the average to be currently employed. Four in ten have no current income. In most respects, this group stands a bit closer to the first need group than to the other two need groups; but two-thirds are under 40 years of age, compared to just one-third of those said to need custodial protection.

The third need group is most easily differentiated from other need groups by the relatively high proportion who are young and are in good health, and by the lower proportion who have been institutionalized. A majority of those who have recently become homeless due to various economic and personal crises or natural disaster are under 30 years of age, and more than four-fifths are under 40. Only one in five has a medical problem said to require a doctor's attention. Thirty-eight percent of this group have been in jail or prison, but this proportion is more than 20 percentage points lower than that of any other need group. Only 13 percent have been hospitalized for a mental health problem, well below the average of 31 percent for the entire homeless population. This group also is somewhat better connected than average with relatives and friends.

Those homeless with crisis care needs are almost as financially deprived as the homeless in other need groups. They are more likely than those in the first two need groups to be working (28 percent) and, if they have any income, are more likely to rely primarily on earned income (31 percent). On the other hand, 30 percent have no current income; of those who do, a majority rely mainly on welfare or, in a few cases, on private charity. The public welfare benefits that these people receive do not prevent their becoming homeless. In fact, the precipitating crisis is often a problem with payment of the rent or an eviction for which there may or may not have been economic reasons. The economic characteristics of this need group suggest, therefore, that besides help in dealing with the crisis triggering their homelessness, many will need ongoing financial assistance or new earned income before they can acquire decent, secure places to live.

The final group in this need hierarchy is the most problematic, since it may contain, in addition to those whose only need is for temporary emergency shelter, some who properly belong in the other categories, but whose service needs are not readily identifiable from the survey responses. Those classified as needing shelter only, are relatively young although not quite as young as the crisis care group. Their other characteristics suggest that they are a highly mobile group, both geographically and in their pattern of employment.

A majority of those classified as needing only emergency shelter have been in the same county for less than one month, a proportion 10 percentage points higher than that of the next most mobile group, those needing developmental services. Their employment pattern also suggests transiency. Compared to the other three need groups, a higher proportion of those classed as needing only shelter have worked in the last month (42 percent); but a nearly equal proportion (43 percent) report no income during that time. Of those in the fourth group with current income, one-half relied primarily on earnings; and a much smaller proportion of this group than of the others relied on transfer payments such as welfare or Social Security. The pattern of erratic or intermittent employment is reinforced by the larger percentages in this group, whose last jobs ended voluntarily or were temporary.

There is some evidence to suggest that the method of classification puts some people in the fourth category who may need developmental or even custodial care. Nearly 20 percent of the fourth group have been in mental institutions at one time or another, a proportion that is well below the average for all homeless but is still sizable. Also, small proportions of those not now working say that their last jobs ended due to poor health (5 percent), poor mental health (6 percent), or drinking or drug problems (4 percent). About one-fourth say they have medical problems that need the care of a doctor. Perhaps 10 to 20 percent of this group, then, might be reassigned to other need categories.

Generally, then, this closer look at the need hierarchy confirms its validity and further illustrates its potential utility as a basis for examining alternative public policies.

CONCLUSION

In recent years, the main focus of debate over policies to aid the homeless has been on the numbers who need and the adequacy of efforts to provide emergency shelter. A more differentiated perspective on the homeless, similar to that taken here, may help to refocus the debate on what is required to make various categories of homeless economically secure and to provide them with stable attachments to other people.

It would be especially helpful if it were possible to estimate what proportion of all homeless in the United States need each form of assistance. The information to determine this simply is not available. However, if the same proportions of the four need groups found in the Ohio homeless population were to hold nationally, then on the order of 100,000 homeless people sleeping in emergency shelters or on the street properly belong in a permanent custodial housing situation where they would receive continuing attention.[2] This is approximately equal to the total number of emergency shelter beds that existed nationally in 1984. The comparison of these two numbers begins to suggest the limits of current public policies for the homeless, policies that are the focus of the next chapter.

NOTES

1. The needs of 39 Ohio homeless could not be established due to missing responses to some items. These are excluded from the analysis reported in this chapter.

2. This number is derived by multiplying the proportion of Ohio homeless needing some form of custodial care by the midpoint number of HUD's "most reliable range" estimate of 250,000 to 350,000 homeless nationally (U.S. Dept. of HUD 1984).

II

PUBLIC POLICY

—— 7 ——

THE EXPANDING EFFORT
TO HELP

In nothing are men more like gods than in coming to the rescue of their fellow men.

Cicero, Marcus Tullius, *Pro Ligario,* 39

In the very short period after 1980, homelessness has moved from the margins of public awareness to centerstage. The media and political leaders have alternately stimulated and responded to rapidly moving public opinion. Viewed not long ago as a chronic and stable feature of urban society, homelessness is now widely regarded as *problematic,* in the sense of being amenable to treatment or prevention, and as an unstable and probably growing phenomenon. From this shift in perception flow new demands for government action to do something about the homeless.

We are very much in the midst of this process of public discovery and the rapid reformulation of perceptions and policy. Today, it is not clear what the new view of the nature of homelessness will prove to be or what symbolic or substantive government actions will satisfy this view. Advocates for the homeless and for other causes compete to define the problem and its solutions. At the same time, public officials and private organizations that raise and spend money for the poor, at all levels, have felt pressure to act, and have responded with expenditures for emergency food, shelter, and other assistance. These actions in turn help redefine the problem by changing the economic and social environment in which the homeless and potentially homeless live.

This chapter examines the expanding public efforts to cope with the "new problem" of homelessness, the new systems of shelter and services, and evalu-

The authors would like to express their appreciation to Kathleen Peroff for her assistance with this chapter.

113

ates this response in light of what we know about causes of homelessness and the needs of this group.

EMERGENCY SHELTER

The nation's emergency shelter capacity has grown rapidly. In major urban areas, the public sector is, for the first time, involved in providing and coordinating shelter and other services for the homeless. A decade ago, operating and funding shelters for the homeless was almost entirely the domain of private religious and other charitable institutions. Nonprofit private groups still operate most (over 90 percent of all) shelters; religious organizations operate about 40 percent of all shelters, while nonreligous groups run the rest.[1] In 1984, fewer than 10 percent of all shelters were operated by city and county governments, almost all of these in New York City. However, public financing of shelters is a new development. Shelter providers report that, in 1983, the public sector (local governments, a few states, and the federal government) provided over $80 million for shelter operation, 37 percent of the total operating costs. The remaining 63 percent was paid by private sources. These figures do not include extensive volunteer labor which, if valued at the minimum wage, amounted to $31 million.

State and local roles

Where the homeless are numerous, local governments have provided more and more resources for shelters. By 1984, four of five city and county governments were involved in some kind of activity to aid the homeless (U.S. Dept. of HUD 1984). New York City, under terms of a court agreement, and Washington, D.C., by voter referendum, are now mandated to shelter all who lack the means to provide it for themselves. Most of the time, local governments do not actually operate shelters but provide subsidies instead to nonprofit groups. Sixty percent of all local governments subsidize shelter operations, and 50 percent provide vouchers to homeless persons for temporary housing. Usually the cost of local services or programs is paid for out of state or federal sources (e.g., the Community Development Block Grant).

The federal government's role

Expansion of shelter capacity and shelter services has been aided primarily by the federal government through its ongoing allocation of HUD community development funds and, since 1983, by annual special congressional appropriations for an emergency food and shelter program administered by the Federal Emergency Management Agency (FEMA). In March 1983, the Congress provided $100 million to this new program; and, in the fall of that year, another

$40 million. For fiscal year 1984, an additional $70 million was appropriated; for 1985, $20 million; and for 1986, another $70 million. The Reagan administration has not supported a separate FEMA program, taking the position instead that such needs are and should be provided for by state and local governments, which can use their own and other federal funds for such purposes. A preliminary and partial accounting of the FEMA program found that the portion of these funds allocated through a national board of charitable organizations, amounting to $91 million, was used to provide 85 million additional meals and 13 million additional nights of lodging.[2] Also, since 1983, $77 million in Community Development Block Grant funds has been used in localities to acquire and rehabilitate buildings for use as shelters, to pay shelter operating costs, or for similar purposes.

Other federal efforts are scattered among several different agency programs and vary in scale and purpose. The total value of various efforts is not known, especially because many involve in-kind benefits (e.g., buildings, space, etc.).

- HUD has encouraged local public housing authorities to provide housing on an "emergency" priority basis to homeless families and elderly individuals. There are no figures on the additional numbers aided as a result, but they are likely to be small. HUD also makes available as shelter for homeless families single-family homes that it has previously acquired due to mortgage default; through the first half of 1985, about 20 such homes had been leased (at a minimal fee of $1 per year) by local governments or private groups for this purpose.

- In 1984, the Department of Defense (DOD) was authorized to make military facilities and incidental services available for shelters for the homeless; through the first half of 1985, DOD had obligated more than $2 million for renovation of its facilities, to be leased to local governments for use as shelters, and had provided blankets and cots for other shelters. For example, the Defense Supply Center in Columbus, Ohio, a federal facility whose operations have been cut back in the last few years, received permission from Washington, D.C., to donate surplus items to local shelters in its area, including tables, chairs, desks, and lockers.

- The Department of Health and Human Services (HHS) has chaired the federal government's Interagency Task Force on the Homeless created in 1983. The task force works as a broker between all federal agencies and local communities to facilitate making federal resources (buildings, equipment, and food) available to local governments. It has, for example, helped to obtain a DOD-owned building and HHS funds for a 400-bed shelter in the District of Columbia. HHS block grants have been used for the homeless, but there are no figures on the dollar amounts. HHS's Alcohol, Drug Abuse, and Mental Health Administration (ADAMHA) has spent $5.6 million for 37 demonstration projects to help homeless persons with mental health, alcohol, or drug problems. HHS also has encouraged states to try innovative ways to provide entitlement benefits to the homeless. Some states are now allowing homeless persons to use a shelter as their "fixed address" in order to receive entitlement benefits.

• The Veterans Administration, the Department of Agriculture, and ACTION are three other federal agencies that, in minor ways, have participated in the federal government's recent effort to help the homeless.

Although many of the programs are small in scale, collectively they constitute a new federal initiative of more than symbolic importance, directed mainly at establishing new shelter capacity in communities across the country.

The shape of a new system

A new system of care-giving for the homeless is emerging. Shelters provide the spatial focus for this network, which encompasses emergency feeding and other services, some aimed at rehabilitation and reintegration. The system of care-giving for the homeless is currently and may well remain a loosely connected, weakly coordinated network, most often with no single locus of authority and accountability at the community level, and with the responsibility for its financing shared by all three levels of government and the private sector.

HUD estimated in the winter of 1984 that there were 111,000 shelter bed spaces nationwide (U.S. Dept. of HUD 1984). This number includes approximately 12,000 for runaway youth, 8,000 for battered or abused women, and 91,000 for all other homeless—single men, single women, and parents with children.[3] These figures do not include those homeless given temporary vouchers for use in hotels, motels, and boarding rooms, although such vouchers account for sizable numbers of persons served, particularly in larger cities such as New York.[4]

Shelter capacity has been expanding rapidly. Four of ten shelters surveyed by HUD had been in operation four years or less; and two in ten had operated for less than one year. All signs point to a continued increase in the number of emergency shelter beds, although they are still less than the number of homeless in many areas.

Rules and requirements

Shelters vary widely in who they will house, the degree to which they impose rules on their occupants, and the length of time they allow a person or family to remain. One shelter in five serves men only (U.S. Dept. of HUD 1984). Slightly smaller proportions accommodate families only and women only. One in four will take in virtually anyone. A small percentage impose more specific restrictions on the types of people they will admit.

Some shelters provide a highly structured environment in which rules are numerous and strictly enforced, while others impose few restrictions. In more structured shelters, occupants may be showered and deloused at entry, smoking may be restricted or prohibited, housekeeping chores may be demanded, and entry may be granted only at certain hours or by advance reservation. Two of three shelters require chores. About one in five requires attendance at religious services, but this proportion is dropping. Even though many of the new shelters are run by churches, attendance at religious services is usually not required. The more structured shelters may not admit and are less attractive than others to people with severe mental illness, with alcohol or drug problems, or with a distaste for rules. The least structured shelters do little to control admission and impose minimal requirements, such as not fighting with other residents or staff, not carrying weapons, and remaining sober. These contrasting operating policies reflect contrasting beliefs about the degree to which structured settings and imposed discipline benefit the homeless. There is a related philosophical division among shelter providers over whether or when occupancy can justly be denied to those who resist the rules but need the shelter.

Most shelters impose some time limit on the number of consecutive nights a person or family can stay. Although the stay limits vary widely from one shelter to another, the average limit is about two weeks (U.S. Dept. of HUD 1984). The range is from no stay limit in New York City's municipal shelters, resulting from a lawsuit brought against the city, to a week or less in some privately operated shelters. About 60 percent of the shelters allow people to remain in the facility around the clock, but the remainder require that all or most occupants leave during daylight hours.

Services

Emergency shelters nearly always provide more than a bed and protection from the weather. Nearly all offer meals and a bath or shower. A large majority provide television, laundry facilities, and clothing. About two-thirds of all shelters provide psychiatric counseling or referrals, and a similar proportion provide job and housing referrals. One-half of the shelters require some form of counseling at admission, although counseling is not always formal or provided by a professional counselor and is more likely to be available in larger shelters and shelters located in larger metropolitan areas.

Because there is typically no close coordination of services provided by different shelters and other agencies, service delivery may be haphazard. In the words of a homeless woman: "One person may have many people all working fruitlessly with her because no one knows of the other person's existence" (McKay 1986, C3).

Short-term care

A few emergency shelters have been recognized as exceptional in the degree to which they attempt to diagnose and meet needs other than the basic needs for food and shelter (see the box following).[5] Short-term facilities that have relatively generous funding can offer a range of help not usually provided in a short-term shelter facility. Some, like the shelter operated by Philadelphia's Committee for Dignity and Fairness for the Homeless, are able to provide professional counseling on a shoestring budget.

The shelter program of Philadelphia's Committee for Dignity and Fairness for the Homeless provides food, lodging, and counseling to more than 40 individuals—men, women, and families—per night. As a matter of policy, the shelter never turns away anyone, regardless of age, sex, or condition. The local Red Cross loans cots to the shelter for a nominal fee. Since no one is turned away, the overflow often must be accommodated by placing a piece of foam and a couple of blankets wherever there is room. Someone skilled in social work or counseling reviews each person in the shelter. After this assessment, the caseworker and the resident agree on a daily task assignment. The caseworker rarely provides direct help. If the resident is unable to accept the responsibility, he or she is usually referred to another service provider for assistance. The shelter's operating budget of about $5,000 per month supports a staff of three full-time and nine part-time workers.

In some places, what were intended only to be short-term emergency facilities have, in effect, become longer-term or permanent residences. This is most likely to occur where there are no length-of-stay restrictions, no service or counseling programs designed to move people out into permanent, independent residences, and where the local government is under legal obligation to guarantee shelter to any homeless person. Through the end of 1985, only New York City was clearly in the latter category. There is reason for concern when facilities intended only for emergency, temporary accommodations and not approaching the minimum standards required for subsidized low-income housing are converted *de facto* to such use. In other places, however, deliberate attempts are being made to develop more adequate long-term facilities for previously homeless persons.

Longer-term care

Longer-term care facilities can put more emphasis on rehabilitation (see the box following). The House of Ruth in Washington, D.C., which shelters women, Seattle Emergency Housing Services, which accommodates families, and the Catholic Charities Parish Shelter program in Chicago, which helps families as well as single men and women, are three examples of this more ambitious and costly approach.

It should be remembered that there are few such longer-term care programs for the homeless in operation today. Those cited here are examples of the most innovative programs of this type.

The House of Ruth in Washington, D.C., provides emergency shelter, two meals a day, clothing, counseling, and employment advice for up to 65 women at a time. No woman in need is ever turned away, meaning that late arrivals often require the use of couches or chairs. On arriving, a guest may be seen by a social worker who helps assess her needs, assets, and plans. This is not mandatory, and residents are not pressured to take counseling. Following intake, each is given a bed, hygiene supplies, night clothes, towels, and washcloths. If desired, a case plan is designed to help resolve the resident's present crisis and eventually to move her toward a more economically stable living situation. Clothing and transportation may be provided for job interviews, medical exams, or appointments with Social Security or public assistance offices. Staff help find jobs and permanent housing and serve as advocates in helping residents qualify for public assistance, rehabilitation, or other public benefits. Many women continue to need a supportive environment with minimal supervision but with continued advocacy and financial support. After a time, some of these are able to live on their own and be financially independent; but many never become totally self-sufficient. Some of these are elderly. Increasing numbers have come to the program with incapacitating mental disabilities. The House of Ruth has an operating budget of $400,000.

The Seattle Emergency Housing Services program began in 1972 as an emergency shelter for families with children. Today, in cooperation with the Seattle Housing Authority and local churches, the program provides transitional housing and related services. The nonprofit agency operates 35 emergency housing apartments (tenure 1–5 weeks) and ten interim housing apartments (tenure 1–4 months) in five Seattle locations. This program helps families break out of homelessness by giving loans of up to $500 for 18 months, at no interest. This money can be used by families in interim housing to pay moving costs, security deposit, and the first month's rent for their own apartment. In 1983, 90 loans were made; the default rate is between 5 and 10 percent. Although no income limit is imposed, most loans are made to those whose living expenses will not exceed 70 percent of family income, including food stamps. Costs for interim housing average $125 per month. Seattle Emergency Housing has an annual budget of $500,000 supported by the City of Seattle, King County, and private contributions.

In Chicago, the Catholic Charities Parish Shelter program provides emergency shelter and transitional housing to families and individuals homeless due to fire, unemployment, or other crises. The program emphasizes casework planning and follow-up. At shelters in three parishes, caseworkers help up to 53 occupants to develop immediate as well as long-term goals for regaining permanent independence. The shelter refers people with special needs, such as abused women or the mentally ill, to other shelters. Entering residents must agree to cooperate with caseworkers. Each resident enters into a contractual agreement *with the shelter, taking personal responsibility for his or her stabilization process. In addition, residents undertake a number of tasks designed to facilitate self-sufficiency. Most meals are prepared by the residents, and they are responsible for cleaning up afterward. Residents are expected to convert to a money order most of the money they receive while staying at the shelter. This money is deposited in a parish account, ensuring that money is saved in preparation for independence. Residents also are expected to attend daily informational meetings and to receive instruction in housekeeping and mini-management skills. The program's annual cash budget is $110,000. Paid professional staff manage the shelter 24 hours a day. In addition, the shelter depends heavily on volunteers and external support from the Catholic Charities' community network.*

Prevention

A few local programs approach the problem of homelessness from a different perspective. Their objective is to reduce the numbers of homeless in the community by finding permanent residences for families and individuals threatened with homelessness, preferably before they are forced onto the street. Such programs can be relatively costly, but their costs may be at least partially offset by the reduced need for emergency shelter capacity in the community (see the box below). The Housing Development and Support program in Worcester, Massachusetts, tries to find permanent housing for its mentally ill clients. In Cleveland, policies of the Cuyahoga County Department of Public Welfare and the Metropolitan Housing Authority have helped to minimize the numbers in need of emergency shelter there.

The Housing Development and Support program of Worcester is intended to help mentally ill homeless through direct housing referrals and social rehabilitation. Begun in late 1983, the program has helped a number of former mental health patients living in the community without supervision move into more adequate housing. Participants must accept instruction in a variety of self-help tasks, including personal hygiene, budgeting, and shopping. Clients are referred to housing judged to be in their individual interests, are helped to secure basic living resources such as bed linens, and may be assisted in developing specific rental agreements with landlords. Often, a contract is made between the client and the community mental health center, under terms of which the client is required to fulfill certain tasks or obligations such as keeping the apartment clean, seeing a therapist regularly, following a medication regime, or going to work. Clients must be willing to see a case manager who constantly monitors progress, watches for signs of illness, and provides intervention in times of crisis. Owners and managers of housing facilities are advised on how to deal with such tenants. The program's director describes it as "the least expensive, least restrictive link in a chain that runs from the state hospital to nursing homes and then to commu-

nity residences.'' But, the program is still "terribly expensive. We have to find cheaper, more effective ways of finding housing.

The American Red Cross in Cleveland, Ohio, counsels individuals and families in emergency shelters to help them find private housing within their means. A few households also are given limited financial aid (for instance, the first month's rent). During 1986, about 125 households (75 individuals and 50 families) were helped in this manner. The Red Cross also has worked with the city's eviction court to counsel and find other help for households about to be made homeless due to lease problems. The program substantially reduces the average length of stay in emergency shelter and, thus, the overall need for shelter space. Dayton and Toledo, Ohio, and Richmond, Virginia, now operate similar programs.

To summarize, the system that is being created for the homeless emphasizes emergency shelter, usually coupled with limited counseling and referrals. A few of the better-financed, more professionally staffed programs make efforts at rehabilitation and reintegration, often in conjunction with other service providers.[6] In some communities, longer-term but still temporary accommodations are available to some homeless. In a few places, special efforts have been made to prevent homelessness, either by addressing proximate causes or by placing people into permanent housing at a point when they otherwise would be forced into emergency shelters or onto the street.

If present trends continue, the system of shelter and services for the homeless is likely to expand further. Congress seems likely to continue annual appropriations for emergency food and shelter, although deficit reduction efforts may undercut this. Private funds, as well as state and local resources, are also likely to increase with heightened public consciousness of this problem. The recent substantial funding, by the Robert Wood Johnson Foundation and the Pew Memorial Trust of health services for the homeless, points to an expanded private sector role. While most non-federal programmatic activity is at the local level, a few states, especially those with large homeless populations, are, for the first time, providing funds for emergency assistance to the homeless.

APPRAISING THE EMERGING SYSTEM

Given the characteristics of the homeless and their apparent service needs, how well are they served by the developing system in communities across the country? This question can be considered in three parts: Does the current system of shelters and shelter subsidies have enough capacity to handle the number of homeless? How well are the service needs of the homeless met by the kinds of shelter-based service programs that have been created? How adequate are present efforts at prevention?

Capacity

The evidence regarding shelter capacity turns out to be quite complex. On the face of it, shelter capacity is not nearly equal to the numbers of homeless. By HUD's count, there are at least two and possibly three times as many people in need of shelter nationally as there are shelter beds.[7] But paradoxically, HUD also found that, during the month of January 1984, the nation's shelters averaged only 70 percent occupancy. This is a surprising discrepancy.

One possible explanation is that shelters are not always located where the homeless are; matching the geographic distribution of shelter capacity with that of the homeless may be impossible because of their mobility. Unfortunately, HUD's national sample of shelters contains too few shelters in any single metropolitan area to allow analysis of variations in shelter occupancy at a metropolitan level. Another possible indication of a mismatch between supply and demand is provided by the statistics on the numbers of people turned away when they seek admittance to a particular shelter. However, interpretation of turnaway statistics is complicated for two reasons: (1) many of those turned away from one shelter may be granted admittance elsewhere on the same night; and (2) people may be turned away from a shelter not because it is full but because they do not fit the admission requirements (e.g., gender, cleanliness, sobriety) imposed by that shelter. HUD's survey shows that the monthly number turned away by the average shelter in January 1984 was far higher in the West (154) than in the Northeast (47), South (27), or North Central (17) regions. Of the four regions, the West has the highest ratio of homeless population to total population, which may indicate that homeless people are being turned away in larger numbers there because more shelters are occupied to capacity. On the other hand, shelter occupancy rates are as high or higher, on average, in the Northeast as in the West. Thus, the statistical evidence is inconclusive.

Even within a given metropolitan area, some shelters may not be fully occupied while people stay on the street for a variety of reasons (U.S. Dept. of HUD 1984). The minimal fees charged by some shelters exclude those homeless who do not have the means to pay or who want to conserve their meager resources for other needs. Others lack information about or access to shelters within their metropolitan area. Some will be excluded from the shelters involuntarily because they cannot cope with the rules imposed or because they represent a threat to others. Additional numbers will exclude themselves voluntarily because they prefer temporary accommodations of their own devising, perhaps in an abandoned building, a wooded area, or even over a steam grate. In better weather, the beach, a park, or a culvert may be preferred for various reasons to the atmosphere and amenities offered by a readily accessible shelter.

The homeless view shelters as varying in congeniality and amenities. Shelters that offer such services as psychiatric counseling, job referrals, and housing referrals have significantly higher occupancy rates than others (U.S. Dept. of HUD 1984). This suggests that many homeless need and are interested in these services and that shelters which offer only an austere protection from the elements may be passed over by some in favor of places that meet a broader range of needs.

Weighing all evidence, there does not appear to be a national shortage of emergency shelter capacity for the homeless, relative to actual demand. At the same time, due to a less-than-optimal geographic distribution of this capacity, there are places and times when homeless people are turned away, with local shortages of shelter capacity most often noted for homeless with special needs, such as runaway youth or the mentally ill. Overall, though, given the rising public and private sector commitment to funding emergency shelter, the expansion of capacity should at least keep pace with any further growth in the homeless population. The mere expansion of shelter capacity does not, however, ensure that the nonshelter needs of the homeless are met. That depends on what goes on inside the shelters and elsewhere.

The match between needs and programs

Today, the shelters contain many who ought to be in permanent custodial settings ranging from in-community sheltered living arrangements to nursing homes, hospitals, or other institutions. In Ohio, roughly one-third of the emergency shelter population belongs in permanent housing arrangements that would provide them with regular if not continuous monitoring and protective care. On the streets, lacking even temporary shelter, there are many more people with this need. In fact, the homeless population not in shelters or other temporary housing probably contains a higher proportion of those needing custodial care than the remainder of the homeless population[8] for two reasons: first, those whose need for such care stems from impaired reasoning are less likely than others to find their way to the shelters; and, second, most shelters cannot provide the close, continuous, and costly attention that this group of homeless requires. Simply expanding shelter capacity will not resolve this mismatch between needs and programs. New programs, representing new approaches, must be created.

For the remainder of the homeless population, a disjuncture between programs and needs is not so apparent. The better shelters (such as those profiled in this chapter) attend to the needs of those homeless who have a deficit or problem requiring rehabilitation services and to the needs of those in crisis for specialized counseling and advocacy; but "most shelters provide little more than a cramped nighttime haven" (Lublin 1986, 1). The emergency shelter system generally fails to provide much for those needing developmental assistance or crisis care.

With regard to those needing developmental services, one relevant piece of evidence is the length of time they remain homeless. In Ohio, for instance, 15 percent of those needing developmental assistance have been homeless for two years or longer without being effectively rehabilitated. To better interpret this statistic, it would be helpful to know the rates at which such people move in and out of homelessness for reasons other than rehabilitation. But, to date, careful longitudinal studies of the homeless necessary to establish this have not been conducted. What is known about the nature of the U.S. social welfare system suggests that many of the homeless who are illiterate, who have physical or mental disabilities requiring specialized rehabilitative therapy, or who have chronic problems with drugs or alcohol will not get the assistance they require to overcome these obstacles to achieving a more stable living situation (cf. Human Services Research Institute 1985). Such treatments are generally expensive, usually provided on a fee basis, and clearly are beyond the means of most in this group, 40 percent of whom have no current income whatsoever.

The present system probably does a better job of meeting the needs of those made homeless temporarily due to a personal crisis or disaster. Crisis care is less expensive and often available without charge, at least for limited periods. The quality of crisis care is likely to vary, depending on the adequacy of specialized facilities and services in a particular community and the efficiency with which the local information and referral network matches needs with available programs.

Finally, the emergency shelter system works best for those homeless whose primary or only need is for temporary accommodations. The only question that arises here is whether it is wiser to house this population under the same roof with those who have additional service needs, as often happens, or to serve these groups in separate facilities.

Prevention

The limitations of the emerging system might be dealt with by adding specialized services or facilities. Another approach altogether, and one with which there is limited experience, is to attempt to reduce homelessness through programs of prevention. The few available examples of aggressive efforts to prevent homelessness (such as the Worcester and Cleveland cases cited in this chapter) offer some encouragement that a prevention strategy could reduce the homeless population and thus the need for spending on shelters, rehabilitation, and reintegration.

CONCLUSION

In the last few years, public and private efforts to deal with homelessness have focused on the most obvious need of the most visible homeless—for protection from the elements. Although many homeless people are still turned away for lack of space in the shelters and a few still die of the cold each winter, the continuing expansion of shelter capacity promises to close the shelter gap soon. But, the public (and private) response should not stop there. The needs of most homeless people are not limited to the basics of food and shelter. If we were to set as our objectives the reintegration into the social mainstream of as many homeless as possible and, better still, the prevention of homelessness wherever possible, the present emergency shelter-based system of care would not be judged an adequate response.

NOTES

1. Many of the statistics in this chapter are drawn from HUD's 1984 report on the homeless and emergency shelters.

2. There are no comparable data on the portion of the FEMA funds allocated to the states.

3. In 1985, New York City alone housed over 20,000 people a night in winter months, including 7,500 single adults and nearly 4,000 families. *New York Times,* November 14, 1985.

4. There is no estimate of the numbers housed with vouchers, but this is a common practice in some localities, especially during periods when occupancy in emergency shelters is near capacity. For instance, the County of Los Angeles, in the winter of 1984, was providing between 2,000 and 4,000 vouchers nightly to shelter homeless in SRO hotels and similar places.

5. The examples cited in this section are documented in U.S. Department of Health and Human Services (1984). Information on the House of Ruth is also provided by Lublin (1986).

6. Lublin (1986) reports that "perhaps 100 or more of the roughly 2,000 U.S. shelters now help some homeless to rejoin society through professional counseling, medical care, job training and placement, and links to permanent housing."

7. HUD's count of the homeless does not include those in temporary paid lodgings or living temporarily with family or friends, some of whom might move to free shelter spaces (does not include the fluctuating numbers of vouchers provided for hotel, motel, or boardinghouse rooms in some localities).

8. In Ohio, about 40 percent of those not in shelters or other housing appear to need custodial care.

8

ALTERNATIVES

Public policy has taken several steps forward since the not-too-distant time when homeless people were, for the most part, either ignored or harassed. Today, public action is mainly focused on providing emergency shelter. Tomorrow, public policy may aim to meet a broader range of needs for this group, by preventing homelessness where possible and by treating it, when it occurs, as part of a larger syndrome of deprivation. Or, the public may lose interest and public policy may aim to make the homeless invisible once again.

No one can forecast how the complex interaction of media images, government policy, the real needs of this population, and the public's responses to these things will reshape the society's relationship with its homeless.[1] It is easy to imagine at least three, very different, scenarios:

SCENARIO 1

The homeless might disappear as an issue. There are several reasons why this is plausible. First, the numbers and visibility of the homeless have only recently crossed the threshold of public awareness that divides major from minor issues. Any decline in their numbers, real or perceived, might put them back below that threshold. Closely related is the extra attention that flows to the homeless because they are perceived as a "crisis," a growing problem of uncertain limits, rather than a chronic but stable social feature. The far larger numbers of the poor and the unemployed do not attract proportionately more attention than the homeless partly for this reason, except when their numbers rise dramatically. If experts and reporters should agree that the numbers of homeless are stable or dropping, awareness may drop sharply and suddenly. Another factor is psychological fatigue. As T. S. Eliot said it, "Mankind cannot stand too much real-

126

ity." Other groups that once attracted comparable attention, such as migrant workers, have dropped from view. But not because their problems were solved; to the contrary, the lack of an obvious or cheap remedy may have contributed to their "disappearance." Also, the relative lack of information about the nature and causes of homelessness give this problem an ambiguity that begs for redefinition. It would serve the political or economic interests of some and relieve the consciences of many others if the phenomenon were redefined in terms that helped return it to relative obscurity.

Harvard University has placed iron grills over heating grates to prevent homeless people from sleeping behind one of its dormitories. Officials at the Cambridge, Massachusetts, campus said the installation of grills at Leverett House was prompted by students' complaints of harassment by street people who congregate on the grates for warmth.

Washington Post, *January 16, 1986*

Columnist George Will: "If it is illegal, and it is, and ought to be illegal, to litter the streets, frankly it ought to be illegal for people who must survive in panhandling among other things to sleep in the streets. Therefore, there is a simple matter of public order and hygiene in getting these people somewhere else. Not arrest them, but move them off somewhere where they are simply out of sight...."

ABC's "Nightline," as quoted in The New Republic, *March 18, 1985*

To make the problem go away does not require that the homeless actually disappear from public view. However, public policies might be pursued that serve to hide the homeless. Removing the most visible groups of homeless from the cities' streets (those acting bizarrely, pushing shopping carts of their belongings along downtown sidewalks, or camped out on busy street corners) would remove most of the visible reminders of this form of deprivation. Selective removal might be accomplished by expanding the legal conditions for confinement of those believed to be mentally ill, by reinstituting the vagrancy laws used not many years ago to clear the streets, or by providing less visible forms of accommodation for the homeless, including more daylight-hour facilities in downtown areas or longer-term residences in remote locations such as closed military bases or summer camps not used in the winter. Examples of each of these forms of removal can be found in some jurisdictions even now. Thus, government policies could be devised to eliminate the most visible part of the problem, thereby reducing pressures for further action and expenditure to meet the needs of the other, less visible, but much larger components of the homeless population. Thus might the society resolve the issue cheaply; but there are other plausible scenarios.

SCENARIO 2

If society stays on its present course, it will continue to build new shelter capacity, of varying physical standards and operated under varying philosophies, ranging from minimal restrictions on the terms and length of occupancy to highly structured and/or rehabilitation-oriented programs for those prepared to accept such a regimen. Limited counseling and other social services will be provided for most shelter occupants, mainly on a voluntary basis. Extrapolating from present trends, we might soon see, in all major urban areas, the creation of a permanent capacity to shelter all or nearly all individuals and families who need and want such shelter.

This has been and is likely to continue to be the primary response to the problems of the homeless because it sets an attainable goal, one that meets the most immediate and obvious need and on which there can be wide agreement. In most communities, it also builds on an existing system of privately run missions and shelters. The operators of these facilities are often the strongest local advocates for the homeless; whereas other human service agencies (welfare, mental health, education) do not have the homeless as their primary clientele and so are directly concerned with only part of that population. Other possible responses, by comparison, may be seen as potentially costly, ineffective, and controversial.

SCENARIO 3

Another scenario, perhaps less likely than the first two, might result from our learning more about the needs of the homeless. A more differentiated view of this population might produce leadership and public support for a new system of services and care, with the goal of minimizing the numbers who, at any one time, are in emergency shelters or without shelter. This might be accomplished, on one hand, by preventing some people from becoming homeless and, on the other, by assisting reintegration of some homeless with the society and providing permanent custodial care for others. The practicality of each element of such an approach, of course, remains to be tested.

The likelihood of this scenario depends not only on whether new approaches prove cost-effective, but also on how they meet the criterion of political feasibility. For example, where the continued expansion of shelter capacity (as in Scenario 2) encounters strong community or neighborhood resistance, political leaders may be attracted to a prevention program that promises to reduce the need for new shelters. Or, where a combination of prevention and custodial care arrangements promises to reduce the visibility of the homeless population, it may appeal to the same interests served by Scenario 1.

Plausible reasons can be found why each of the three scenarios is likely. There is little question, however, that the first two scenarios would be far less beneficial to the homeless than the third, provided that an array of cost-effective programs can be created and funded that go beyond shelter to meet other needs. These would include prevention efforts; custodial care for those who cannot return to independent living; as well as developmental services and crisis help as needed to foster a return to more normal living. The remaining task, then, is to examine these alternatives with the knowledge we have at hand, beginning with prevention.

THE LIMITS OF PREVENTION

The belief that prevention is inherently more cost-effective than treatment after the onset of a malady, whether social or physical, has been influential, especially in recent years, in the fields of health and mental health.

Prevention strategies often fail to live up to their initial appeal, however, for several reasons. A strategy aimed at *primary* prevention (i.e., before the onset of a problem) may encounter difficulty in identifying those most at risk and in reaching them in the most timely way. We have noted the complex and variable etiology of homelessness. Although institutionalization for mental illness puts a person at risk of being homeless after release, only a very small fraction of all deinstitutionalized persons actually become homeless. Although extreme poverty contributes directly to homelessness, only a few of the poor are actually homeless at any one time. If the response to the difficulty of early identification is to intervene in broader fashion (e.g., by raising the incomes of all poor or regularly monitoring the housing conditions of all those released from institutions), then the problems become ones of cost and public acceptance. Many must be helped to avoid what only a few would have experienced. In addition, some primary prevention strategies addressed to homelessness would involve major changes in social structure and the role of government that have implications far beyond the issue of homelessness.

In the near term, therefore, the strategies likely to be cost-effective in reducing the incidence of homelessness are those that offer *secondary* prevention, that is, interventions that occur at or soon after the time when a person or family loses a home. If effective, such actions would shorten the duration of homelessness and reduce the numbers who eventually wind up on the streets, thus minimizing the degree of deprivation experienced in terms of time and place. If successful, prevention programs such as those described in the preceding chapter would shorten the average stay in emergency shelters, freeing space for others and ultimately reducing the shelter capacity required in a community or across the country.

What would a prevention strategy involve? By what standards would its success be measured? How likely is it to succeed? What are the limits of efforts to reduce the incidence and duration of homelessness?

To return people to independent living as quickly as possible requires a combination of services aimed not just at locating housing but at meeting other needs.

These could include establishing a stable source of income, working through a crisis in personal relationships, or finding day care for children. Help in finding permanent housing could involve a combination of housing counseling, transportation, help in meeting landlords or housing authorities and completing applications, budget planning, and help in locating appropriate vacancies.

This can take some time. For example, people in 17 Massachusetts shelters seeking housing took an average of 3.5 months to find a place to stay; and some of these went on to live with friends or in other shelters. The average search time actually exceeded the maximum length of stay most of the shelters allowed by policy (Cooper 1985). Not all of these shelters provided the kinds of intensive housing search assistance described above, and many of the searchers had been homeless for quite a while before they reached that shelter. It would be useful to know whether search times can be reduced when more help is provided and when intervention occurs earlier.

A cost-effective secondary prevention effort would pay for itself in reduced shelter operating costs and capital cost savings due to the reduced need for shelter space. For example, a program that reduced the average length of stay by 15 days for 100 people at $20 per bed-night (which is close to the national average cost) would save $30,000 annually in shelter operating expense—about enough to cover the salary of one housing counselor. Capital cost savings could more than offset other program costs. Such programs could more easily generate net savings where there is a sizable underutilized stock of low-cost housing. Where the supply of low-cost housing is more constrained, a program providing modest rent supplements to households not eligible for federal housing assistance may be necessary, and thus the possibility for net savings would be reduced.[2]

Prevention programs of this sort do not address the needs of most of those who have been homeless for some time. They are most appropriate for those who have recently become (or are about to become) homeless via an eviction, disaster, or personal crisis and who need limited help to reestablish a normal living pattern. They do not, by themselves, meet the needs of that fraction of the homeless population who should be in permanent custodial settings; nor do they apply, unless supplemented by other forms of help, to the homeless who need developmental services. Finally, they are irrelevant to those who are voluntarily homeless, whether for short spells or as a way of life. While prevention efforts deserve far more attention than they have received, it is very unlikely (given what we know about this population) that most cases of homelessness can be prevented or brought to an early end in this way.

REINTEGRATION

Whether prevention efforts could significantly reduce the homeless population or not, our analysis of their service needs suggests that a large proportion might return to a normal living pattern if given appropriate services—short-term crisis care in some cases and longer-term developmental services in others. In Ohio, roughly one-half of the homeless are in one of these two need categories.

It is unlikely that new service programs for the homeless will have very high success rates or that they will pay for themselves by reducing the need for shelter capacity. Some of these efforts will be very expensive. They must be justified, if at all, on the basis of their benefit to the homeless and their broader benefit to the society. Two hundred years ago, Dr. Samuel Johnson observed that, ultimately, the test of civilization was to be found in the way it treated its poor. Starkly, the choice is between a system of emergency shelter and minimal services aimed at maintaining life and limb and a far more ambitious effort to help people return to the kind of life we, and they, consider normal.

Developmental service needs are those required to overcome barriers to economic self-sufficiency and to create a capacity for independent living. In addition to help directed at remedying deficits such as illiteracy or alcohol and drug abuse, these efforts must involve counseling and close, temporary supervision designed to reverse behavior patterns that evolved as an adaptation to homelessness but would only produce rejection by employers or landlords. The largest part of the homeless population needing developmental services are those who have serious problems with alcohol or drugs. Virtually nothing is known about the latter group. About the alcoholic homeless, there is some new, but still very incomplete, insight regarding what may be required (Wittman 1985).

Detoxification programs for alcohol-dependent destitute and homeless people in New York City have produced few successful rehabilitations (Sadd 1985). James Wright (1985) concludes that: "the best detoxification and counseling program in the world will have little success if, at the end of treatment, the door swings open and the client returns once again to life on the streets" (p. 27). In other words, there is little prospect for success unless alcohol rehabilitation is part of a larger effort to remove homeless people permanently from their present environment.

A new approach to this task is being tried in San Francisco and is serving as a model for other communities. This is the creation of a "sober hotel," where the formerly homeless alcoholic can be partially shielded from pressures to continue drinking. The first such hotel provides a long-term alcohol-free residence for 174 recovering alcoholics. Its few simple rules include absolutely no alcohol or nonprescribed medications on the premises, careful housekeeping, and attendance at house meetings. No formal therapy is provided on site, but residents give one another peer support. The management arranges for backup health, mental health, or social services as needed. Operation is said to cost between $12,000 and $30,000 annually per bed, higher than the $7,000 or so national average cost of a shelter bed but far lower than the $100,000 per bed cost of jail or the $200,000 per bed cost of hospitals (Clark 1985). However, it is too soon to establish the effectiveness of this promising step toward a reintegration strategy for the homeless alcoholic.

Another group in need of developmental services are those homeless who lack the work experience, basic education, and marketable skills needed to be economically self-sufficient. Benefit levels in most states for individual adults (i.e., those eligible only for general assistance or SSI) are far lower than required to purchase modest but decent and physically standard housing. And, we have seen that, for various reasons, many of those eligible for this assistance have no source of income or have followed a pattern of intermittent, temporary day labor or other marginal employment.

To be reasonably self-sufficient and therefore able to pay for housing, these homeless must be returned to the active labor force and be capable of obtaining and retaining full-time employment. Many are functionally illiterate. Some have never worked. As with programs for alcoholics, experience with programs designed to move such adults from the margins into the mainstream of the society shows that they are often expensive and not necessarily cost-effective. Based on the recent history of efforts to help a variety of people become self-sufficient, the single adult homeless person with no recent history of steady employment may be a relatively poor prospect for such programs (Burtless and Haveman 1984). However, while programs directed at the hard-to-serve generally have lower success rates than those directed at people who are more "job ready," the former also tend to produce greater average net gains per individual when controlling for how well people would do in the absence of the program (Gueron 1985).

A rapidly expanding number of states and communities are experimenting with various mixes of education, training, required or voluntary work experience, and supportive services—all addressed to the large problem of how to move people toward economic self-sufficiency. Prominent examples are New York State's Temporary Employment Assistance Program (TEAP) for general assistance recipients, Massachusetts's "ET" program, Florida's "Trade Welfare for Work" program, and HUD's "Project Self-Sufficiency," the latter involving over 100 localities. Although some of this new activity follows earlier models, much of it is innovative and directly applicable to the segment of the homeless population for whom economic self-sufficiency will require a substantial investment in education and supportive services.

The Job Corps provides one model for this kind of reintegration effort. Features that make it potentially attractive for the homeless include total separation from the disorganizing influence of the homeless habitat and an emphasis on educational remediation, practical skills training, and resocialization. Although costly to implement, the Job Corps model also has the potential to produce greater benefits, judging from its results with disadvantaged youth, than cheaper but less comprehensive, in-community approaches (Taggart 1981). However, its success depends on a degree of personal commitment that many homeless people may be unwilling or unable to give it.

If such an effort is to take place within the community, then it must confront the challenge of providing intensive remediation and reorientation in an environment that constantly threatens to undermine that learning process. At a minimum, it seems essential to first stabilize the living situation of the individual. A person moving frequently from one emergency shelter to another or living on the street is not a good prospect for reemployment. Ideally, therefore, a specialized intermediate-term facility should be created to house the participants. For the skills training itself, an attractive model is offered by programs, such as the Ventures in Community Improvement demonstration, which use the work site to provide occupational skills training as a transition to jobs in construction (Corporation for Public/Private Ventures 1980). Such programs could be combined with, and would complement, spending for the rehabilitation of older buildings for use as emergency shelters.

New York's TEAP program, providing on-the-job training, is of special interest because it is directed at general assistance recipients (single adults) who were initially categorized as "unemployable." In its first two years, over one-half of the participants who completed the training period were retained by their employers; and many others immediately moved to other jobs. Even among those who did not complete training, "a considerably higher percentage were found to be employed during the subsequent six months than . . . among a comparable group of non-TEAP . . . recipients" (O'Neill 1985, 153–54). This program, and a similar state program in Minnesota, are exceptional in their focus on general assistance recipients and encouraging in their early results.

Unfortunately, single adults without children comprise most of the homeless with this set of service needs; and they are ineligible for many remediation and training programs, which are tied to AFDC. Also, few local Job Training Partnership Act programs give priority to single adults who have minimal education and work experience (Noble 1985). Thus, existing programs that may be appropriate for the homeless would have to be expanded or equivalent programs would have to be created and funded, perhaps by state governments, before this range of needs could be met fully.

CUSTODIAL CARE

A sizable fraction of the homeless population (in Ohio, about 30 percent) will continue to be homeless unless they are given some kind of sheltered living arrangement. This does not, in most cases, mean institutional confinement. For most, it implies a congregate or other sheltered living arrangement, in the community, combined with specialized supportive services. For some, it may mean an independent, self-maintained residence with continuous close monitoring by others.

The homeless who need these kinds of permanent care arrangements include those with severe chronic mental illness, who are approaching normal retirement age, who are physically incapable of regular employment, or who have been homeless and unemployed for so long that there is little probability of their return to a normal pattern of independent living.

At present, "the number of programs specifically designed to assist those who are both mentally ill and homeless are woefully inadequate in relation to need" (Levine 1984). For instance, fewer than one-fourth of the Ohio homeless who show signs of severe psychopathology have been in contact recently with a community mental health program.

There is much to learn about the most effective way to care for such people. Research indicates that the kinds of comprehensive, coordinated, and accessible services systems demonstrated by the federal government's Community Support Program (CSP) can improve conditions for the chronically mentally ill (Market Facts 1981; Tessler and Goldman 1982). To help those who are homeless, however, the CSP approach must be modified significantly. Altered outreach, more attention to housing and other basic needs, and special sensitivity by providers to the attitudes and circumstances of the homeless are among the modifications required for this population (Levine, Lezak, and Goldman unpublished; Ball and Havassy 1984).

One likely source of new information is a joint effort of the Robert Wood Johnson Foundation and the U.S. Department of Housing and Urban Development announced at the end of 1985. The foundation is contributing $28 million in grants and loans and the department has promised 1,000 rental assistance certificates and $4.5 million in contract authority to assist in organizing a strengthened system of community mental health services, better coordinating these with other city services, and purchasing and/or rehabilitating properties suitable for sheltering the chronically mentally ill. As many as eight major cities will participate.

Rather than hospitalization, the homeless mentally ill in most cases need community-based care (Human Services Research Institute 1985); however, this will require development and funding of new community care approaches. The creation of such programs in a large number of places is likely to be hampered by a lack of funding and staff for community mental health programs (Levine and Stockdill 1986, 15) and by the limited supply of housing subsidies.

The shortage of subsidized housing is acute in many places, despite a steady expansion in the numbers assisted.[3] This shortfall affects the prospects for providing sheltered living arrangements to all homeless in need of custodial care. Many of these are single adults below the minimum age (62) that would make them eligible for subsidized housing although they may qualify if they are found to be disabled. Because there have been no longitudinal studies of the homeless, we can only speculate that a high proportion of those in their fifties, who have been on the streets for a long time and often have serious health problems, will not survive long enough to become eligible for this housing. They need to be in custodial care now; but the likelihood that local housing authorities will or can alter their priorities to accommodate this group seems low. Thus, a solution appears to require further expansion of housing subsidies for the very poor, especially for congregate facilities where those who have been homeless and destitute for years can be given the attention they need.

If the prospects of meeting the custodial care needs of these homeless seems small, it is important to recognize the spending that is associated with the present situation, in which many of the aging and disabled homeless spend an increasing portion of their existence in and out of hospital emergency rooms and out-patient facilities and claim a disproportionate share of attention from the staff of emergency shelters not designed to accommodate this range of needs.

BAD IDEAS

Every bad precedent originated as a justifiable measure.

Sallust, *Bellum Catilinae*, LI, 27

Frustration with the inadequacy of present efforts to aid the homeless has led some to advance ideas that, if implemented, might do more harm than good. One set of ideas, that we need new laws to protect some homeless from themselves, threatens the civil liberties of many others. Another bad idea, that government should sanction the creation of cheap substandard housing for the homeless, would break precedent with the long-held goal of bringing all U.S. housing to one minimum standard.

In 1985, the public debate over policies related to the homeless shifted toward questions of compulsion and rights. The two specific issues being discussed were: whether cities, like New York, could forcibly remove homeless people from the streets on cold nights, on the presumption they were incompetent; and whether homeless people with diagnosed psychopathology should be institutionalized against their will, on the grounds that they were a danger to themselves. Both raise constitutional issues and run counter to the trend of judicial opinion in recent decades.

Forced sheltering

New York City's policy of forced sheltering illustrates the first of these issues (see PBS, "MacNeil/Lehrer News Hour," December 23, 1985). In the winter of 1984–85, Mayor Koch ordered that, when the windchill factor fell below 5°F, homeless people without a source of shelter and apparently disoriented were to be taken to public hospitals for examination. The following winter, the mayor amended this order, requiring removal of these homeless to hospitals when temperatures fell below freezing (32°F).

New York City's procedure for forced sheltering works as follows. A police officer on the beat encounters a homeless person without shelter in below-freezing weather. If the officer believes that the homeless person is incompetent to make a judgment on his or her own behalf, he then calls a police sergeant who will determine whether the person is incompetent and in need of shelter. If the sergeant makes a positive determination, then the homeless person is taken, by force if necessary, to a psychiatric facility where a psychiatric professional assesses the individual's mental competency. If found incompetent, then the person is taken, against his or her will if necessary, to a public shelter. The few homeless thus detained have been released the next day.

The moral argument for such a policy has been captured by Charles Krauthammer (1985, 104):

> There is a reason for forcibly removing the homeless mentally ill from the streets: not society's fear of what the homeless are doing to us, but concern about what they are doing, cannot help doing, to themselves. In a society that aspires to be not only free but humane, removing the homeless mentally ill should be an act not of self-defense but of compassion.

However, pressures on local officials from interests such as businesses and residents might lead them to expand the scope of a forced removal policy to include other people under other circumstances.

A case against forced removal has been presented by the New York City chapter of the American Civil Liberties Union (ACLU). The ACLU argues both legal and practical considerations in protecting the homeless from forced sheltering by the state (see PBS, ''MacNeil/Lehrer News Hour,'' December 23, 1985). Although the ACLU accepts the legal right of the state to provide protective care for those who are mentally incompetent, it cannot accept the lack of due process of law.[4] Under U.S. law, depriving a person of rights for protective purposes requires that the person be represented by counsel before a court. There are no exceptions. The ACLU argues that the homeless do not give up their rights because they are homeless but have all of the rights guaranteed to any citizen.

To this argument Krauthammer responds:

> Liberty counts for much, but not enough to turn away from those who are hopelessly overwhelmed by the demands of modern life. To permit those who flounder even in the slowest lane to fend for themselves on very mean streets is an act not of social liberality but of neglect bordering on cruelty. In the name of a liberty that illness does not allow them to enjoy, we have condemned the homeless mentally ill to die with their rights on.

To which another participant in this debate might reply (Mitchell 1986):

> The law means well. All laws mean well. The authors of the Constitution, whatever else may be said of them, had a hearty distrust of guys . . . going about doing good.

The freedom not to be carted off by cops without a specific warrant, or the presence of a crime, is an important freedom. It should not be fiddled with simply because in some rare case it might be a good thing.

Reinstitutionalization

At present, most states allow involuntary civil commitment only if an individual can be demonstrated to be "potentially dangerous" to himself or others. In practice, this requires that objectively verifiable criteria be used before commitment is ordered. Usually, the criteria err on the side of noncommitment when difficult cases are encountered. Critics of deinstitutionalization would like to see the standards for commitment relaxed so that many of the homeless mentally ill could be moved "off the streets ... and back in facilities designed for people in their condition" (Perkins 1985).

Recently, the pendulum has begun to swing back in favor of looser commitment standards, a situation prevalent before the 1970s. The American Psychiatric Association's new model law (Holden 1985), for example, proposes that states reject the "potentially dangerous" criterion and replace it with the concept of "significant deterioration" or "grave disability." This alternate concept focuses on whether the person is capable of tending to his or her physical needs rather than on his potential dangerousness. It might also permit institutionalization of people who were not yet, but likely to become, gravely disabled. In addition to shifting the grounds for institutionalization, this broader standard would place decisions regarding commitment much more in the hands of the medical rather than the legal community.

Like the issue of forced shelter, the movement to broaden the grounds for institutionalization has implications not only for the homeless but for the rights of other citizens (see Holden 1985, 1253–55, for a review).

The "potential danger" criterion came into use because of concern generated by flagrant rights abuses occurring in the commitment of people to mental hospitals. Individuals often were not afforded due process under the law, including the right to counsel, to receive treatment, and to expect some limited duration of stay. Moreover, some viewed the typical mental hospital not as a place for rehabilitating people but as a warehouse for stockpiling them, often for an indefinite period. The criterion of "potential danger" forced the judicial system to commit only the most severe and unambiguous cases to the hospital system; and, once they were there, forced operators to provide some minimal treatment.

Those now favoring broader criteria have argued that the stricter standards are forcing people onto the streets who are dangerous—if not at the time of their commitment hearing then later. Once there, they say, most of these people not only do not receive treatment, but are a source of danger and disturbance. In December 1985, CBS reported that a woman was unable to have her daughter committed to an institution, despite the fact that she had been diagnosed as schizophrenic and for several years was living on the streets of New York as a "bag lady." The daughter continues to live alone on the streets, tormented by internal voices that give her no peace. In another broadcast by all three television networks at about the same time, reporters told of a homeless 19-year-old woman, deinstitutionalized against her doctor's orders, who pushed a passenger waiting for a subway to her death. Also in late November 1985, the mass media carried a story of a homeless woman who walked into a Wall Street trading firm and killed the owner. The woman, a former mental patient, reportedly believed she was part-owner of the firm and was being cheated. The conclusion that some draw from these cases is that the standards for commitment are too loose and that too many people who should be institutionalized are harming themselves and others.

Civil libertarians counter that these are isolated cases (Holden 1985) and that no one knows for certain or can readily determine the likelihood that an individual will be in danger if left free. Turning the arguments of those who favor a looser standard against them, civil libertarians have responded that if the current strict standards for commitment cannot sort out those who need or do not need treatment, then looser standards will suffer from the same inexactitude. As with forced sheltering, the potential for broader harm seems to outweigh any possible benefits to the homeless mentally ill or others.

Shacks

Drawing a lesson from the squatters camps of poorer nations, Leland Burns (1986) has proposed that U.S. public officials legalize such encampments and "turn a blind eye to building- and occupancy-code violations" in such places. This would provide a relatively cheap solution to the housing needs of a group that clearly is not being served by other government housing programs.

This modest proposal sees similarity between America's homeless and the squatters in San Salvador's *tegurios*, Rio de Janeiro's *favelas*, and Ankara's *gecekondus*. "In the developing nations, the key to unlocking the latent energies of the homeless was the discovery that prevailing views about squatters were substantially incorrect. Instead of the rascals and radicals that they were presumed to be, they were simply poor people, bewildered by the complexities of urban life. Given the opportunity, they had substantial potential for upward mobility (Burns 1986). Resistance to this idea is likely from "public servants whose job it is to make and enforce codes." Burns notes that one federal public housing official, asked why American Indians "had to be housed at prevailing, middle-class standards when relaxed standards would have produced housing for more families," responded: " 'We don't want to be accused of building second-class housing for second-class citizens.' " Burns's answer to this is: "Do it we must."

It would be easier to dismiss this idea as one having no application to the United States if there were no examples of government involvement in creating second-class housing for the homeless. However, in New York, where the average stay in the public shelter system has reached 11 months (Crystal and Goldstein 1984) and where individuals and families may remain indefinitely in welfare hotels that are physically inadequate and dangerous, government is deeply involved in the *de facto* creation of a new second-class form of public housing. Besides the direct harm done by holding people for long periods in facilities not designed as permanent residences, this trend violates a basic tenet of U.S. housing policy in the modern era: that the goal should be to provide everyone with housing that meets the same basic standards. We have certainly fallen short of this goal as a society, but we have not so far abandoned it.

The bad ideas have a common thread. The homeless are in a special category, to which the usual protections and standards of treatment do not apply. This is a dangerous strain of thinking that could harm not just the homeless, but many others.

RESPONSIBILITIES

Fashioning an effective response to the needs of the homeless is a responsibility shared by governments at the local, state, and federal levels and by the private nonprofit services sector. A response that is locally designed and administered stands a better chance of matching the particular character of the problem in that locality. On the other hand, the very uneven geographic distribution of the homeless population and variations in local capacity and willingness to address the needs of that population suggest a role for higher levels of government. In addition to providing financial support for impacted localities, the state and federal levels of government possess the critical mass of resources and expertise required to support policy innovation. Given the fiscal constraints on action at the federal level, the states may be in a better position to sponsor innovative programs and their evaluation.

At the community level, an effective response to the varied needs of the homeless population will require new mechanisms to coordinate services for this group. Responsibility for this coordination probably should not rest with a single shelter or service agency, since each deals with an unrepresentative fraction of the homeless population and may hold a specialized professional perspective. Given their highly successful performance in administering a portion of the FEMA emergency food and shelter program and their tradition of coordinating a diverse group of services at the community level, local United Ways may be the appropriate forum within which to organize a coordinated services reponse to homelessness. Two agencies that have played major parts in helping the homeless, the Salvation Army and the Red Cross, are generally under the United Way umbrella. Public welfare agencies and community mental health centers also must play a coordinating role if a coherent system of services is to be created.

Centralization of responsibility at the local level is a virtual prerequisite for the establishment of procedures to ensure that the homeless receive services appropriate to their needs. These procedures should include a comprehensive individual needs analysis and continuous tracking of service provision and its results. Since many of the homeless have multiple service needs, the timing and delivery of help by various agencies should be centrally managed. Since this is a highly mobile population, both within and between communities, shelters and other providers must be prepared to share information about their clients, given their informed consent. Since the homeless frequently cross jurisdictional boundaries, state governments should authorize and encourage the exchange of information across localities.

States should lead in creating a coordinated system of services for the homeless at the community level. States also should sponsor and support demonstration efforts to meet the differentiated needs of the homeless, including prevention programs, crisis care and counseling, developmental services for those on general assistance and SSI as well as AFDC, and an array of in-community custodial care arrangements. These demonstrations should be carefully evaluated and the best ones used as models for permanent state or federally funded programs.

A LOOK AHEAD

No one could look at the alternatives before us and be sanguine about the prospects for dealing humanely and adequately with the needs of the American homeless.

One goal is within reach, however: the creation of enough shelter space. The nation, collectively, spends about $300 million annually to operate emergency shelters; each year, it invests more capital to expand and improve this system. The society thus is close to providing at least a minimum of shelter to everyone who needs it.

Even the least adequate emergency facilities offer a measure of rest and a meal to those who have hit bottom. The best offer much more. But, if we accept the creation of a permanent massive shelter system as the main response to homelessness, then we accept also the permanence of a large population with no place to call home. If we accept this as a solution, we accept our failure to develop effective approaches to prevention, our abandonment of reintegration as a goal for most of the homeless who need special help to live independently, and our failure to create new permanent custodial settings for those who have been debilitated by poverty and life on the streets. If, out of frustration or embarrassment in the presence of so many who are so obviously suffering, we acquiesce in measures that deny them the same rights and protections as others, then we do potential harm to ourselves as well as to them.

To meet more than the basic immediate needs of the homeless, we must look beyond the provision of shelter to other approaches. Efforts to prevent homelessness or reduce its duration look like they could significantly diminish the need for shelter and thus perhaps pay for themselves. For others who have been made homeless, more costly and in many cases untried approaches are required to meet their needs for crisis care or for rehabilitation, education, and other support in becoming economically independent. And finally, for a sizable fraction of the homeless population, the humane alternative to life outside or inside shelters is permanent protective care. If we recognize that these are the different needs of various groups of homeless, then the creation and funding of these alternatives ought to be the long-range goals of public policy.

NOTES

1. For an illuminating treatment of how the actions of government interact with the psychological needs expressed through public opinion, readers should see Murray Edelman, *The Symbolic Use of Politics* (1964).

2. The Maryland Governor's 1986 housing initiatives include a proposed pilot program of rental allowances for homeless persons who qualify for general assistance but are ineligible for federal housing subsidies (Maryland 1986).

3. At the end of 1985, about four million poor households lived in subsidized privately and publicly owned housing, compared to about three million five years earlier.

4. The ACLU also argues that Mayor Koch's program, however justified in the abstract, is highly problematic when applied. They have claimed that: (1) homeless people report that police officers are not following the procedures laid down in Mayor Koch's decree. In many cases, officers have threatened people with violence unless they willingly board buses; (2) homeless people across the country have indicated that they are afraid of shelters because of the potential dangers these facilities hold for them. Many shelters house together in a small space people with problems including physical disease, drug abuse, mental illness, and vermin, and exhibiting disturbing, violent, or criminal behavior. Since the state cannot guarantee their individual safety, homeless people should not be compelled to place themselves in jeopardy; and (3) New York has insufficient capacity to deal with homeless people who voluntarily seek assistance at public shelters.

BIBLIOGRAPHY

Alter, Jonathan. 1984. "Homeless in America." *Newsweek*, January 2.

Anderson, Kurt. 1983. "Left Out in the Cold." *Time*, December 19.

Arce, A. A., M. Tadlock, M. J. Vergare, et al. 1983. "A Psychiatric Profile of Street People Admitted to an Emergency Shelter." *Hospital and Community Psychiatry* 34: 812–17.

Bachrach, Leona L. 1982. "Conceptual Issues in the Evaluation of the Deinstitutionalization Movement." *Innovative Approaches to Mental Health Evaluation*, edited by G. J. Stahler and W. R. Tash (New York: Academic Press), pp. 139–61.

——. 1983. "Planning Services for Chronically Mentally Ill Patients." *Bull Menninger Clinic* 47: 163–88.

——. 1984a. "The Homeless Mentally Ill and Mental Health Services: An Analytical Review of the Literature." In *The Homeless Mentally Ill*, edited by H. Lamb (Washington, D.C.: American Psychiatric Association), Chapter 2.

——. 1984b. *Report and Analytical Summary of a Meeting of DHHS-Supported Researchers Studying the Homeless Mentally Ill* (Rockville, MD: National Institute of Mental Health).

Ball, F. L. J. 1982. *San Francisco's Homeless Consumers of Psychiatric Services: Demographic Characteristics and Expressed Needs* (San Francisco Community Health Services, May), photocopied.

Ball, F. L. J. and B. E. Havassy. 1984. "A Survey of the Problems and Needs of Homeless Consumers of Acute Psychiatric Services." *Hospital and Community Psychiatry* 35: 917–21.

Bane, Mary Jo and Michael J. Dowling. 1985. *Trends in the Administration of Welfare Programs*. Paper presented to the 1985 Annual Meeting of the Association for Public Policy Analysis and Management, October 26, Washington, D.C.

Bane, Mary Jo and David T. Ellwood. 1983. *The Dynamics of Dependence: The Routes to Self-Sufficiency* (Cambridge, MA: Urban Systems Research and Engineering, Inc., June).

Barrow, S. and A. M. Lowell. 1982. *Evaluation of Project Reach Out, 1981–82* (New York: New York State Psychiatric Institute, June 30), photocopied.

Bassuk, E. L. 1983. "Addressing the Needs of the Homeless." *Boston Globe Magazine*, November 6, pp. 12–60ff.

——. 1984. "The Homeless Problem." *Scientific American* 251: 40–45.

Baxter, E. and K. Hopper. 1981. *Private Lives/Public Spaces: Homeless Adults on the Streets of New York City* (New York: Community Service Society).

——. 1982. "The New Mendicancy: Homeless in New York City." *American Journal of Orthopsychiatry* 52: 393–408.

Beattie, Richard I. and Richard J. Tofel. 1984. "Understanding Who is Homeless in New York City." *New York Times*, December 1.

Berger, Joseph. 1985. "Failure to Plan for Homeless Reflects City Housing Crisis." *New York Times*, February 19.

Bernard, Leon. 1970. *The Emerging City, Paris in the Age of Louis XIV* (Durham, NC: Duke University Press).

Boston Emergency Shelter Commission. 1983. *The October Project: Seeing the Obvious Problem* (Boston, MA: City of Boston, October).

Brown, C., S. MacFarlane, R. Paredes, et al. 1983. *The Homeless of Phoenix: Who Are They? And What Should Be Done?* (Phoenix, AZ: Phoenix South Community Mental Health Center).

Burns, Leland S. 1986. "Third-World Models for Helping U.S. Homeless." *Wall Street Journal*, January 2.

Burt, Martha R. and Lynn C. Burbridge. 1985. *Major Findings: Evaluation of the Emergency Food and Shelter Program* (Washington, D.C.: The Urban Institute).

Burtless, Gary and Robert H. Haveman. 1984. "Policy Lessons from Three Labor Market Experiments." In *Employment and Training R & D: Lessons Learned and Future Directions*, edited by R. Thayne Robson (Kalamazoo, MI: W.E. Upjohn Institute for Employment Research).

Buss, Terry F. and F. Stevens Redburn. 1985. *Long-Term Effects of a Plant Closing* (Columbus, OH: Ohio Department of Mental Health).

California Department of Housing and Community Development. 1985. *A Study of the Issues and Characteristics of the Homeless Population in California* (April).

Chmiel, A. J., S. Akhtar, and J. Morris. 1979. "The Long-Distance Psychiatric Patient in the Emergency Room." *International Journal of Social Psychiatry* 25: 38–46.

Clark, Wayne. 1985. "Financial and Developmental Aspects of Housing for the Homeless with Alcohol-Related Problems." In *The Homeless with Alcohol-Related Problems*, edited by F. D. Wittman (Rockville, MD: National Institute of Alcohol Abuse and Alcoholism), pp. 12–16.

Committee for Creative Non-Violence (CCNV). 1982. *Homeless in America* (Washington, D.C.).

Consortium for the Homeless. 1983. *The Homeless of Phoenix: Who Are They? And What Should Be Done?* (Phoenix, AZ: June).

Cooper, Nancy. 1985. *After Shelters: Providing Permanent Housing for Homeless Families and Individuals* (Boston, MA: Citizens Housing and Planning Association, October).

Corporation for Public/Private Ventures. 1980. *Enhanced Work Projects—The Interim Findings from the Ventures in Community Improvement Demonstration* (Washington, D.C.: U.S. Government Printing Office, May).

Crystal, Stephen, et al. 1982. *Chronic and Situational Dependency: Long-Term Residents in a Shelter for Men* (New York: Human Resources Administration, May).

Crystal, S. and M. Goldstein. 1984. *Correlates of Shelter Utilization: One-Day Study* (New York: Human Resources Administration).

Depp, F. C. and V. Ackis. 1983. *Assessing Needs Among Sheltered Homeless Women*. Presented at the Conference on Homelessness: A Time For New Directions, Washington, D.C., July 19.

Dohrenwend, Bruce P., et al. 1978. "The Psychiatric Status Schedule as a Measure of

Dimensions of Psychopathology in the General Population.'' *Archives of General Psychiatry* 33: 731–37.

Downs, Anthony. 1983. *Rental Housing in the 1980s* (Washington, D.C.: The Brookings Institution).

Eberts, Randall W. 1984. ''Components of Employment Change in Cleveland.'' *REI Review* 2 November, pp. 3–12.

Edelman, Murray. 1964. *The Symbolic Uses of Politics* (Champaign/Urbana, IL: Illini Books).

Farr, R. K. 1982. *Skid Row Project* (Los Angeles, CA: Los Angeles County Department of Mental Health, January 18), photocopied.

Foucault, Michel. 1965. *Madness and Civilization* (New York: Pantheon; originally published in France in 1961).

Freeman, Richard B. and Brian Hall. 1986. ''Permanent Homeless in America'' (Cambridge, MA: National Bureau of Economic Research), photocopied.

Goldman, H. H., A. A. Gattozzi, and C. A. Taube. 1981. ''Defining and Counting the Chronically Mentally Ill.'' *Hospital and Community Psychiatry* 34: 129–34.

Gueron, Judith M. 1985. *Testimony Before the Intergovernmental Relations and Human Resources Subcommittees of the Committee on Governmental Relations*. U.S. House of Representatives, July 9.

Halpern, Joseph, et al. 1980. *The Myths of Deinstitutionalization* (Denver, CO: West view Press).

Harris, Lyle V. and John Mintz. 1985. ''For Area's Homeless, Battle is to Stay Warm.'' *Washington Post*, December 29, p. A9.

Harris, M. and H. C. Bergman. 1983. ''Youth of the '60s.'' *Hospital and Community Psychiatry* 34: 1164.

Hauch, Christopher. 1985. *Coping Strategies and Street Life: The Ethnography of Winnipeg's Skid Row*. Report #11 (Winnipeg, Canada: Institute of Urban Studies, University of Winnipeg).

Himmelfarb, Gertrude. 1984. *The Idea of Poverty: England in the Early Industrial Age* (New York: Alfred A. Knopf).

Holden, Constance. 1985. ''Broader Commitment Laws Sought.'' *Science* 230: 1253–55.

Hombs, Mary Ellen and Mitch Snyder. 1982. *Homelessness in America: A Forced March to Nowhere* (Washington, D.C.: Community for Creative Non-Violence).

Human Resources Department. 1982. *New Arrivals: First Time Shelter Clients* (New York: City of New York, June).

——. 1983. *Monthly Shelter Report* (New York: City of New York, December).

——. 1984. *New York City Plan for Homeless Adults* (New York: City of New York, April).

Human Services Research Institute. 1985. *Homelessness Needs Assessment Study* (Boston, MA: Massachusetts Department of Mental Health).

Jensen, Arthur R. 1980. *Bias in Mental Testing* (New York: Free Press).

Job, Barbara C. 1979. ''How Likely are Individuals to Enter the Labor Force?'' *Monthly Labor Review* 102 (September): 28–34.

Kasinitz, Philip. 1984. ''Gentrification and Homelessness: The Single Room Occupant and the Inner City Revival.'' *Urban and Social Change Review* 17 (Winter): 9–14.

Kates, Brian. 1985. *The Murder of a Shopping Bag Lady* (New York: Harcourt, Brace, Jovanovich).

Kerr, Peter. 1985. "Suburbs Struggle With Rise in the Homeless." *New York Times*, December 22.

Kondratas, S. Anna. 1985a. "A Strategy for Helping America's Homeless." *The Backgrounder* 431 (Washington, D.C.: Heritage Foundation, May 6).

———. 1985b. "How Many Homeless: The Numbers Game Is Ridiculous." *Los Angeles Times*, July 18.

Krauthammer, Charles. 1985. "When Liberty Really Means Neglect." *Time*, December 2, pp. 103–104.

Lamb, H. R. 1982a. "The Mentally Ill in an Urban County Jail." *Archives of General Psychiatry* 40: 363–68.

———. 1982b. *Treating the Long-Term Mentally Ill: Beyond Deinstitutionalization* (San Francisco, CA: Jossey-Bass).

———. 1982c. "Young Adult Chronic Patients: The New Drifters." *Hospital and Community Psychiatry* 33: 465–68.

———. (ed.). 1984. *The Homeless Mentally Ill* (Washington, D.C.: American Psychiatric Association).

Leo, John. 1985. "Harassing the Homeless." *Time*, March 11, p. 68.

Levine, Irene S., Anne Lezak, and Howard H. Goldman. Unpublished manuscript. *Developing Community Support Systems for the Homeless Who are Seriously Mentally Ill* (Washington, D.C.: National Institute of Mental Health).

Levine, Irene S. 1984. "Service Programs for the Homeless Mentally Ill." In *The Homeless Mentally Ill*, edited by R. Richard Lamb (Washington, D.C.: American Psychiatric Association).

Levine, Irene S. and James W. Stockdill. 1986. "Mentally Ill and Homeless: A National Problem." In *Treating the Homeless: Urban Psychiatry's Challenge,* edited by Billy Jones (New York: American Psychiatric Association Press).

Lewis, N. 1978. *Community Intake Services for the Transient Mentally Disabled (TMD)* (San Francisco, CA: Traveler's Aid Society of San Francisco), photocopied.

Lublin, Joann S. 1986. "Some Shelters Strive to Give the Homeless More Than Shelter." *Wall Street Journal*, February 7, pp. 1–6.

Main, Thomas J. 1983a. "The Homeless of New York." *The Public Interest* 72: 3–28.

———. 1983b. "New York City's Lure to the Homeless." *Wall Street Journal*, September 12.

Manpower Demonstration Research Corporation. 1980. *Summary and Findings of the National Supported Work Demonstration* (Cambridge, MA: Ballinger).

Market Facts, Inc. 1981. *Collaborative Data Collection and Analysis for Community Support Program Demonstration Projects* (Rockville, MD: National Institute of Mental Health).

Maryland, State of. 1986. *Meeting Today's Challenge and Building for the Future: The Governor's Housing Initiatives of 1986* (Annapolis, MD).

McElvaine, Robert S. 1983. *Down and Out in the Great Depression.* (Chapell Hill: University of North Carolina Press).

McKay, Pia. 1986. "My Home Is a Lonely Bed in a Dreary D.C. Shelter." *Washington Post*, February 16, pp. C1–C3.

Mitchell, Henry. 1986. "Cold Facts About Our Civil Rights." *Washington Post*, January 3.

Morse, Gary, Nancy M. Shields, C. R. Hanneke, R. J. Calsyn, G. K. Burger, and B.

Nelson. 1985. *Homeless People in St. Louis: A Mental Health Program Evaluation, Field Study, and Follow-up Investigation*, Vol. 1 (Jefferson City, MO: State of Missouri, Department of Mental Health).

New York Department of Social Services. 1984. *Homeless in New York State: A Report to the Governor and the Legislature* (October).

New York State Office of Mental Health. 1982. *Who Are the Homeless? A Study of Randomly Selected Men Who Use New York City Shelters* (Albany, NY: May).

Newman, Sandra J. and Ann B. Schnare. 1985. *Reassessing Shelter Assistance: The Interrelationship Between Welfare and Housing Programs*. A paper presented to the Seventh Annual Research Conference of the Association for Public Policy Analysts and Management, Washington, D.C.

Noble, Kenneth B. 1986. "Study Finds 60% of 11 Million Who Lost Jobs Got New Ones." *New York Times*, February 7, pp. A1–A15.

———. 1985. "U.S. Job Training Programs Rouse Bitter Disputes." *New York Times*, March 25.

O'Neill, Hugh. 1985. *Creating Opportunity: Reducing Poverty Through Economic Development* (Washington, D.C.: Council of State Planning Agencies).

O'Neill, June, Douglas A. Wolf, Laurie J. Bassi, and Michael T. Hannan. 1984. *An Analysis of Time on Welfare* (Washington, DC: Urban Institute, June).

Ohio Department of Mental Health. 1985. *Homelessness in Ohio: A Study of People in Need* (Columbus, OH: February).

Palmer, John L. and Isabel V. Sawhill. 1984. *The Reagan Record* (Cambridge, MA: Ballinger Publishing).

Peele, R. and R. R. Palmer. 1980. "Patient Rights and Patient Chronicity." *Journal of Psychiatry and Law* 8 (Spring): 59–71.

Perkins, Joseph. 1985. "New Institutions for the Homeless." *Wall Street Journal*, February 26.

Priest, R. G. 1976. "The Homeless Person and the Psychiatric Services." *British Journal of Psychiatry* 128: (February), 128–36.

———. 1971. "The Edinburgh Homeless: A Psychiatric Survey." *American Journal of Psychotherapy* 25, no. 2: 194–213.

Public Technology, Inc. 1985. *Caring for the Hungry and Homeless* (Washington D.C., June).

Rabkin, Judith G. 1979. "Criminal Behavior of Discharged Mental Patients." *Psychological Bulletin* 86 (January): 1–26.

Reich, R. and L. Siegel. 1978. "The Emergence of the Bowery as a Psychiatric Dumping Ground." *Psychiatry Quarterly* 50: 191–201.

Robertson, M., R. Ropers, and R. Boyer. 1984. *Emergency Shelter for the Homeless of Los Angeles County* (Los Angeles, CA: UCLA School of Public Health).

Roth, Dee and Jerry Bean. 1985. "Alcohol and Homelessness: Findings from the Ohio Study." In *The Homeless with Alcohol-Related Problems*, edited by Friedner D. Wittman (Rockville, MD: National Institute on Alcohol Abuse and Alcoholism).

Sadd, Susan. 1985. "The Revolving Door Revisited: Public Inebriates' Use of Medical and Non-Medical Detoxification Services in New York City." In *The Homeless with Alcohol-Related Problems*, edited by F. D. Wittman (Rockville, MD: National Institute of Alcohol Abuse and Alcoholism), pp. 12–16.

Segal, S. P. and J. Baumohl. 1980. "Engaging and Disengaged: Proposals on Madness and Vagrancy." *Social Work* 25: 358–65.

Segal, S. P., J. Baumohl, and E. Johnson. 1977. "Falling Through the Cracks: Mental Disorder and Social Marginality in a Young Vagrant Population." *Social Problems* 24: 387–400.

Spitzer, R. L., J. Endicott, and J. Cohen. 1970. "The Psychiatric Status Schedule: A Technique for Evaluating Psychopathology and Impairment in Role Functioning." *Archives of General Psychiatry* 23: 41–55.

Spitzer, R. L., J. Endicott, J. Cohen, and J. Nee. 1980. "The Psychiatric Status Schedule for Epidemiological Research." *Archives of General Psychiatry* 37: 1193–97.

Spradley, James P. 1980. "Adaptive Strategies of Urban Nomads: The Ethnoscience of Tramp Culture." In *Urban Life*, edited by G. Gmelch and W. P. Zenner (New York: St. Martins), pp. 328–47.

Stein, Mark A. 1985. "Homeless People Publicize Potty Shortage." *Los Angeles Times*, December 14.

Streltzer, J. 1979. "Psychiatric Emergencies in Travelers to Hawaii." *Comprehensive Psychiatry* 20: 463–68.

Tabler, D. L. 1982. *Preliminary Report: Emergency Adult-at-Risk Shelter: A BCDSS Demonstration Project* (Baltimore, MD: Baltimore Department of Social Services, September 20), photocopied.

Taggart, Robert. 1981. *A Fisherman's Guide: An Assessment of Training and Remediation Strategies* (Kalamazoo, MI: W. E. Upjohn Institute for Employment Research).

Taylor, Paul. 1986. "The Coming Conflict as We Soak the Young to Enrich the Old." *Washington Post*, January 5.

Tessler, R. C. and H. H. Goldman. 1982. *The Chronically Mentally Ill: Assessing Community Support Programs* (Cambridge, MA: Ballinger).

Thomas, Jo. 1985. "The Homeless of Europe: A Scourge of Our Time." *New York Times*, October 7.

"Toledo Police Losers in Attempts to Change Life Style of 'Bag Lady.' " 1985. *Youngstown Vindicator*, September 1.

U.S. Alcohol, Drug Abuse, and Mental Health Administration. 1983. "The Homeless." *ADAMHA News*, June 24.

U.S. Bureau of the Census. 1980. *Geographical Mobility: March 1975 to March 1979* (Washington, D.C.: U.S. Government Printing Office).

——. 1983. *Current Population Reports*. Series P-60. no. 147, *Characteristics of the Population Below the Poverty Level: 1983* (Washington, D.C.: U.S. Government Printing Office).

U.S. Conference of Mayors. 1984. *Emergency Food, Shelter, and Energy Programs* (Washington, D.C.: U.S. Conference of Mayors, January).

——. 1986. *The Growth of Hunger and Homelessness and Poverty in America's Cities in 1985* (Washington, D.C.: U.S. Conference of Mayors).

U.S. Congress, House Committee on Banking, Finance, and Urban Affairs and House Committee on Government Operations. 1984. *HUD Report on Homelessness, Joint Hearing* (Washington, D.C.: May 24).

U.S. Department of Health and Human Services. 1984. *Helping the Homeless: A Resource Guide* (Washington, D.C.: DHHS, September).

U.S. Department of Housing and Urban Development. 1984. *A Report to the Secretary on the Homeless and Emergency Shelters* (Washington, D.C.: Office of Policy Development and Research).

U.S. General Accounting Office (GAO). 1985. *Homelessness: A Complex Problem and the Federal Response* (Washington, D.C.: GAO, April 9).

U.S. Senate. 1983. *Special Hearing on Street People* (Washington, D.C.: U.S. Government Printing Office).

Waxman, Laura D. and Lilia M. Reyes. 1986. *The Growth of Hunger, Homelessness and Poverty in America's Cities* (Washington, D.C.: U.S. Conference of Mayors, January).

Wiegand, R. Bruce. 1985. "Counting the Homeless." *American Demographics* 7: 34–37.

Winograd, Kenneth. 1982. *Street People and Other Homeless—A Pittsburgh Study* (Pittsburgh, PA: Emergency Shelter Task Force, August).

Wittman, Friedner D. 1985. *The Homeless with Alcohol-Related Problems* (Rockville, MD: National Institute on Alcohol Abuse and Alcoholism, U.S. Department of Health and Human Services).

Wright, James. 1985. "The Johnson-Pew 'Health Care for the Homeless' Program." In *The Homeless with Alcohol-Related Problems*, edited by F. D. Wittman (Rockville, MD: National Institute of Alcohol Abuse and Alcoholism), pp. 12–16.

INDEX

ABOUT THE AUTHORS

F. Stevens Redburn is a senior analyst in the Division of Policy Studies, Office of Policy Development and Research, U.S. Department of Housing and Urban Development. Since 1979, he has helped to design and manage a series of national studies addressing current housing and community development policy problems. His most recent books are: *Revitalizing the American Economy* (co-edited with Terry Buss and Larry Ledebur; published by Praeger) and *Mass Unemployment: Plant Closings and Community Mental Health* (co-authored with Terry Buss; published by Sage). His other publications have dealt with economic development, industrial policy, housing, and a broad range of issues in urban policy and public administration. He holds a Ph.D. in political science from the University of North Carolina at Chapel Hill.

Terry F. Buss is director of the Center for Urban Studies at Youngstown State University. Taking advantage of his location in America's distressed industrial heartland, he has published several books and many articles on a variety of public policy issues including mass unemployment, human service delivery, labor markets, economic development, and human capital resources. He is now at work on two separate books, one concerning the long-term effects of plant closings and the other on discouraged workers. He received his doctorate in political science and mathematics from Ohio State University in 1976.